D0534109

Nick Vandome

Android Tablets for Seniors

2nd Edition

Covers Android 5.0 Lollipop

In easy steps is an imprint of In Easy Steps Limited
16 Hamilton Terrace · Holly Walk · Leamington Spa
Warwickshire · United Kingdom · CV32 4LY
www.ineasysteps.com

Copyright © 2015 by In Easy Steps Limited. All rights reserved. No part of this book may be reproduced or transmitted in any form or by any means, electronic or mechanical, including photocopying, recording, or by any information storage or retrieval system, without prior written permission from the publisher.

Notice of Liability
Every effort has been made to ensure that this book contains accurate and current information. However, In Easy Steps Limited and the author shall not be liable for any loss or damage suffered by readers as a result of any information contained herein.

Trademarks
All trademarks are acknowledged as belonging to their respective companies.

In Easy Steps Limited supports The Forest Stewardship Council (FSC), the leading international forest certification organisation. All our titles that are printed on Greenpeace approved FSC certified paper carry the FSC logo.

FSC
www.fsc.org
MIX
Paper from
responsible sources
FSC® C020837

Printed and bound in the United Kingdom

ISBN 978-1-84078-649-1

Contents

1 Introducing Android Tablets 7

About Tablets 8
About Android 12
Tablet Terms Explained 14
Using a Touchscreen 16
Using Apps 18
Makes and Models 20
Android and Google 22
Creating a Google Account 24
Turning On and Controls 26
Battery and Charging 27
Setting Up Your Tablet 28
Adding Accessories 30

2 Getting Started with Your Tablet 31

Viewing the Home Screen 32
Navigating Around 33
Adding Apps 34
Moving Apps 35
Working with Favorites 36
Adding Widgets 37
Changing the Background 38
Notifications 39
Creating Folders 40
Screen Rotation 41
Quick Settings 42
Accessing Settings 43
Locking Your Tablet 46
Searching 48
Ok Google 51
Using Google Now 52

3 At Your Fingertips 57

The Android Keyboard 58
Keyboard Settings 60
Keyboard Shortcuts 62
Adding Text 64
Working with Text 65
Creating a Dictionary 66

4 Working with Apps 67

About Android Apps 68
Built-in Apps 69
Around the Play Store 72
Finding Apps 74
Downloading Apps 76
Deleting Apps 78
Updating Apps 79
App Information 80

5 Useful Apps 81

Staying Organized 82
Being Productive 84
Keeping Entertained 86
Lifestyle 88
Health and Fitness 92
Family History 96

6 Tablet Entertainment 97

Using Google Play 98
Music on Android 99
Downloading Music 100
Transferring Music 102

Playing Music 104
Managing Music 107
Pinning Music 108
Movies and TV Shows 110
Obtaining Books 114
Around an Ebook 116
Adding Notes 118
Adding Bookmarks 120
Definitions and Translations 121
Using Cameras 122
Adding Photos 124
Viewing Photos 127
Editing Photos 130
Sharing Photos 132

7 Keeping in Touch 133

Email on Android 134
Adding Email Accounts 135
Using Email 137
Email Settings 139
Social Networking 140
Keeping an Address Book 142
Using Your Calendar 144
Using Your Google Account 146

8 Browsing the Web 147

Android Web Browsers 148
Opening Pages 149
Bookmarking Pages 150
Links and Images 152
Using Tabs 153
Being Incognito 154
Browser Settings 155

9 On Your Travels 157

Traveling with Your Tablet 158
Keeping Your Tablet Safe 160
Airport Security 161
Finding Hotels and Flights 162
Calling with Skype 164
Useful Travel Apps 166

10 Sharing with the Family 169

About Multiple Users 170
Adding Family Members 172
Switching Between Users 174
Guest Users 175
Restricted Profiles 176

11 Accessibility and Security 177

Accessibility 178
Security Issues 180
About Antivirus Apps 181
Using Antivirus Apps 182
Locating Your Tablet 184

Index 187

1 Introducing Android Tablets

Tablet computers and the Android operating system are an ideal match for anyone who wants their computing as mobile and as flexible as possible. This chapter introduces the basics of Android tablets and shows how to get started with them.

8 About Tablets
12 About Android
14 Tablet Terms Explained
16 Using a Touchscreen
18 Using Apps
20 Makes and Models
22 Android and Google
24 Creating a Google Account
26 Turning On and Controls
27 Battery and Charging
28 Setting Up Your Tablet
30 Adding Accessories

About Tablets

Tablet computers are the result of the desire for our computing devices to become smaller and more portable (from desktops, to laptops, to tablets) and the evolution of mobile operating systems, initially introduced for smartphones. The combination of the two has resulted in the birth and relentless march of the tablet; they are small, portable for almost any situation, customizable and powerful enough to perform most everyday computing functions, such as email, using the Web, word processing and communicating with social networking sites.

Android is now owned by Google.

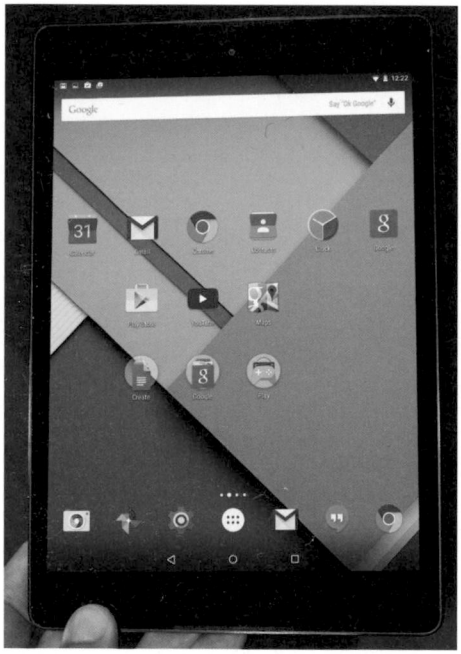

The New icon pictured above indicates a new or enhanced feature introduced with the latest version of Android 5.0 Lollipop for tablets.

Tablets are essentially small computers that run on a mobile operating system, rather than those used on desktop and laptop computers, such as Windows and Mac OS X. They can be used as an addition to your suite of computing products or they could even be considered as a replacement for items such as desktop computers or laptops, depending on your computing needs. But for most types of mobile computing tasks, tablets are definitely the new kid on the digital block.

Android operating system

All computers need an operating system to make them work and perform all of the required tasks for the user. For tablets, the two main operating systems are iOS for Apple tablets (the iPad and iPad Mini) and Android. The latter has been developed through its use on smartphones and is now a significant player in the tablet market. The fact that it is used on both types of device means that if you have an Android smartphone then an Android tablet is a perfect match.

Microsoft Windows can also be used on tablets and Microsoft has its own tablet, the Surface, which uses Windows.

Android is an open source operating system which means that developers and manufacturers can work with the source code to tailor it to their own needs and devices (as long as they meet certain requirements and standards). Android tablets are made by a number of different manufacturers and, although the hardware differs between devices, the Android operating system is common between them (although the versions of Android differ between devices; see page 13). Android tablets generally come in 7-inch to 10-inch models.

For more information about specific makes and models of Android tablets see pages 20-21.

It is now apps instead of programs

The functionality of tablets can be expanded almost endlessly through the inclusion of apps: computer programs that either come pre-installed or can be downloaded from a linked service. For Android tablets, this service is provided by the Google Play Store which is accessed from the tablet (or the Google Play website, which is available with a Google Account; see pages 24-25 for details about creating an account). Some models of tablet also have their own proprietary online store for buying apps, but they will also have the Play Store which, generally, will have a larger range of apps available.

Apps are denoted by the thumbnail icons that appear on the tablet's Home screen (and also in the All Apps area).

...cont'd

Touchscreen

Tablets are touchscreen devices, which means that their functionality and controls are accessed by tapping, swiping or pressing on the screen. This includes the keyboard, which appears on the screen if data input is required, e.g. for writing an email, entering a website address or filling in an online form. For people who have always used a physical keyboard, the virtual one can take a bit of getting used to, particularly if you are doing a lot of typing, but the more you use it, the more familiar it will become.

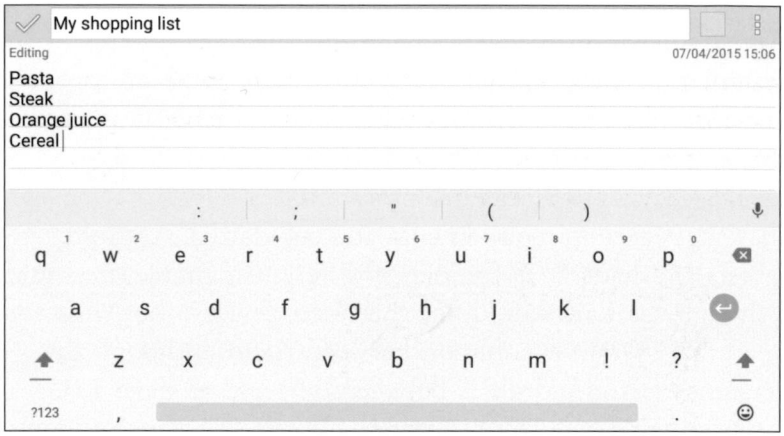

If your tablet has 3G/4G connectivity, you will have to pay for this service from an appropriate provider, in the same way as obtaining Internet access for a smartphone. Only some models of tablet have this type of connectivity.

Getting connected to the Internet

One of the essential functions of tablets is online connectivity, for accessing the Web and also the range of Android services that are connected to Google apps and online services.

The standard form of online connectivity for tablets is provided by Wi-Fi. This will connect to the Internet via your own Wi-Fi router and service provider in your home, or through a Wi-Fi hotspot if you are traveling with your tablet. Some models of tablets also have 3G/4G connectivity. This is wireless, mobile access to the Internet, provided by telecoms companies through either a monthly plan or pay-as-you-go options. This provides access to the Internet without the need for using Wi-Fi.

Hybrid tablets

In computing terms, the current tablet market is a relatively new one and manufacturers are developing ideas in terms of the evolution of the tablet, particularly in relation to the more traditional laptop. Nothing stays the same forever and this is exaggerated in the computing world where change can be particularly fast. Just as the laptop has taken over from the desktop as the main computing device for the majority of people, so the tablet is beginning to make people think about the next stage in the evolution of personal computing and how we interact with the digital world.

Some manufacturers have developed hybrid tablets that are designed to bridge the gap between tablets and laptops. These devices can be used as self-contained tablets, using the virtual, touchscreen, keyboard, or they can be docked to a physical keyboard and be used more like a laptop.

As the tablet market develops and evolves further it is likely that there will be more hybrid models and, in time, tablets could begin to replace laptops for a lot of our mobile computing needs.

The removable keyboards that come with hybrid tablets are not as sturdy as those on a traditional laptop and their size is usually restricted to the width of the tablet.

About Android

Android is essentially a mobile computing operating system, i.e. one for mobile devices such as smartphones and tablets.

Android is based on the flexible and robust Linux operating system and shares many similarities with it.

Android is an open source operating system, which means that the source code is made available to hardware manufacturers and developers so that they can design their devices and apps in conjunction with Android. This has created a large community of Android developers and also means that Android is not tied to one specific device; individual manufacturers can use it (as long as they meet certain specific criteria) which leads to Android being available on a variety of different devices.

Android Inc was founded in 2003 and the eponymous operating system was initially developed for smartphones. Google quickly saw this as an opportunity to enter the cell phone and computing market and bought Android in 2005. The first Android-powered smartphone appeared in 2008 and since then has gone from strength to strength. Android-based smartphones have a majority of the worldwide market and, with the increasing popularity of tablets, it is likely that those running Android will soon experience a similar level of success.

The main differences between the Android operating system and desktop- or laptop-based ones such as Windows or Mac OS X are:

- **No file structure**. There is no built-in File Manager or Finder structure for storing and managing files. All content is saved within the app in which it is created.
- **Self-contained apps**. Because there is no file structure, apps are generally self-contained and do not communicate with each other.
- **Numerous Home screens**. Rather than just one Desktop, there are numerous Home screens on an Android tablet and they can be used to store and access apps.
- **Content is saved automatically as it is created**.

Updating Android

Since Android is open source and can be used on a variety of different devices, this can sometimes cause delays in updating the operating system on the full range of Android devices. This is because it has to be tailored specifically for each different device; it is not a case of 'one size fits all'. This can lead to delays in the latest version being rolled-out to all compatible devices. The product cycle for new versions is usually six to nine months.

Since Android is a Google product, their own devices are usually the first ones to run the latest version of the software. Therefore, the Google Nexus 9 has been the first tablet to come with the latest version of Android, i.e. 5.0 Lollipop, while others are still running previous versions, usually 4.3 Jelly Bean, or 4.4 KitKat or earlier. (*Correct at the time of printing.*) For recently-released tablets, an upgrade to the latest version of Android will be scheduled into the update calendar. However, for some older Android tablets, and smartphones, the latest version of the software is not always made available. This can be because of hardware limitations but there have also been suggestions that it is a move by hardware manufacturers designed to ensure that consumers upgrade to the latest products.

The version of the Android operating system that is being used on your tablet can be viewed from within the **System > About tablet** section of the **Settings** app. This is where the operating system can also be updated when a new version is available.

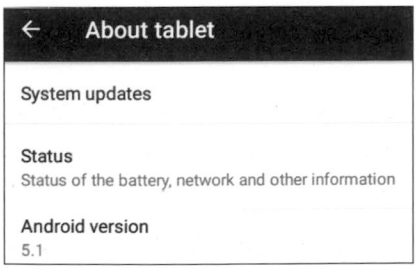

Updated versions of Android are named alphabetically after items of confectionery, e.g. 1.5 was Cupcake and 1.6 was Donut; 4.1, 4.2 and 4.3 were Jelly Bean and 4.4 was KitKat.

The latest version of Android is 5.0 Lollipop. This is available on the Google Nexus 9. However, most other Android tablets are sold with Android 4.2, 4.3 or 4.4, at the time of printing. This book covers Android 5.0 Lollipop on the Google Nexus 9.

Tablet Terms Explained

As with any computing device, there is a significant amount of jargon that can be used in relation to tablets. Much of this is similar to that used for desktop and laptop computers, while some is more specific to tablets themselves.

- **Processor**. Also known as the central processing unit, or CPU, this refers to the processing of digital data as it is provided by apps (programs) on the tablet. The more powerful the processor, the quicker the data is interpreted.

- **Memory**. This closely relates to the processor and is also known as random-access memory, or RAM. This type of memory manages the apps that are being run and the commands that are being executed. The greater the amount of memory there is, the quicker apps will run. With more RAM they will also be more stable and less likely to crash. In the current range of tablets, memory is measured in megabytes (MB) or gigabytes (GB).

- **Storage**. This refers to the amount of digital information that the tablet can store. In the current range of tablets, storage is measured in gigabytes. There are no external signs of processor or memory on a tablet but the details are available from within the **Device > Storage** section of the **Settings** app.

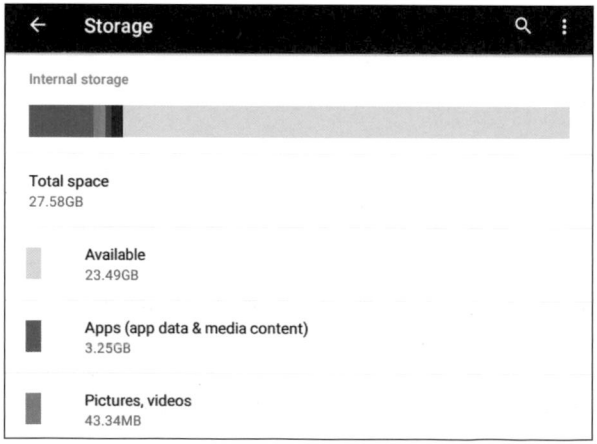

- **Operating System (OS)**. This is what links together the hardware and software of the tablet and gives it its functionality. Android is the operating system that is used on a range of different models of tablets and is the one widely used throughout the world.
- **Connectivity**. This refers to how the tablet connects to the Internet. This is either by Wi-Fi via a compatible router or through mobile access using 3G or 4G, which requires the use of an appropriate, paid-for, service.
- **Graphics card**. This is a device that enables images, video and animations to be displayed on the tablet. It is also sometimes known as a video card. The faster the graphics card, the better the quality the relevant media will be displayed at.
- **Wireless**. This refers to a tablet's ability to connect wirelessly to a network, usually via Wi-Fi.
- **Ports**. These are the parts of a tablet into which items can be plugged, such as the micro USB cable for charging the tablet or connecting it to a computer, an HDMI port for connecting the tablet to a high definition TV and the headphone jack.
- **Camera**. Most tablets have one, or two, built-in cameras that can be used to take stills photographs or communicate via video with other people. There is usually a front-facing camera on most tablets, for video calls, and some also have a rear-facing one for taking higher quality photos and videos.
- **Sensors**. These include a gyroscope for auto-rotating the tablet when it is moved from landscape to portrait and a GPS sensor.
- **Apps**. These are the programs on the tablet. See pages 18-19 for more details.
- **Touchscreen**. See pages 16-17 for details.

Wi-Fi is the most common way to connect wirelessly to the Internet on tablets. This is done by connecting with a wireless network access point, such as a public wireless hotspot, or your own home router.

Using a Touchscreen

The traditional method of interacting with a computer is by using a mouse and a keyboard as the input devices. However, this has all changed with tablets; they are much more tactile devices that are controlled by tapping and swiping on the touchscreen. This activates and controls the apps and settings on the tablet and enables you to add content with the virtual keyboard that appears at the appropriate times.

Gently does it

Touchscreens are sensitive devices and only require a light touch to activate the required command. To get the best out of your touchscreen:

- Tap, swipe or press gently on the screen. Do not use excessive force and do not keep tapping with increasing pressure if something does not work in the way in which you expected. Instead, try performing another action and then returning to the original one.
- Tap with your fingertip rather than your fingernail. This will be more effective in terms of performing the required operation and better for the surface of the touchscreen.
- For the majority of touchscreen tasks, tap, press or swipe at one point on the screen. The exception to this is zooming in and out on certain items (such as web pages), which can be done by pinching inwards and outwards with thumb and forefinger.
- Keep your touchscreen dry and make sure that your fingers are also clean and free of moisture.
- Use a cover to protect the screen when not in use, particularly if you are carrying your tablet in a jacket pocket or a bag.
- Use a screen cloth to keep the screen clean and free of fingerprints and smears. The touchscreen should still work if it has fingerprints and marks on it, but it will become harder to see clearly what is on the screen.

Touchscreen controls

Touchscreens can be controlled with three main types of actions. These are:

- **Tapping**. Tap once on an item, such as an app, to activate it. This can also be used for the main navigation control buttons at the bottom of the touchscreen, or for items such as checkboxes when applying settings for specific items.

- **Pressing**. Press and hold on an item on the Home screen to move its position or place it in the **Favorites Tray** at the bottom of the screen.

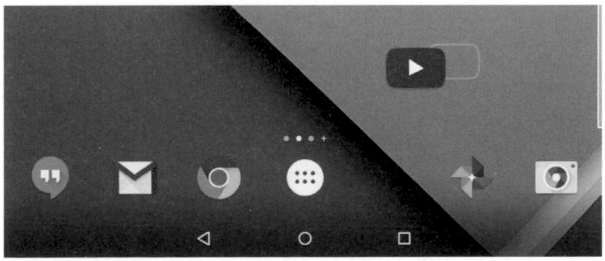

- **Swiping**. Swipe down from the top of the Home screen to access the **Notifications Area** and the **Quick Settings** and swipe up from the bottom of the screen to access the **Google Search** box.

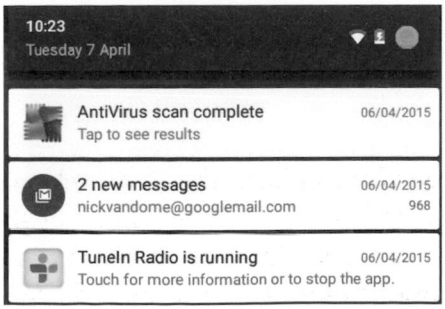

For more information about working with apps on the Home screen, the Notifications Area and the Quick Settings, see Chapter Two.

Using Apps

One of the great selling points for Android tablets is the range of apps that is available from third-party developers. Because Android is open source it is relatively easy for these developers to write apps for Android devices. At the time of writing there are approximately 1.3 million Android apps on the market. Some are free while others have to be paid for.

The built-in apps are the ones that give the initial functionality to your tablet and include items such as email, web browser, calendar, calculator and maps. They appear as icons on your tablet's Home screen, or in the All Apps area, and are accessed by tapping lightly on them once.

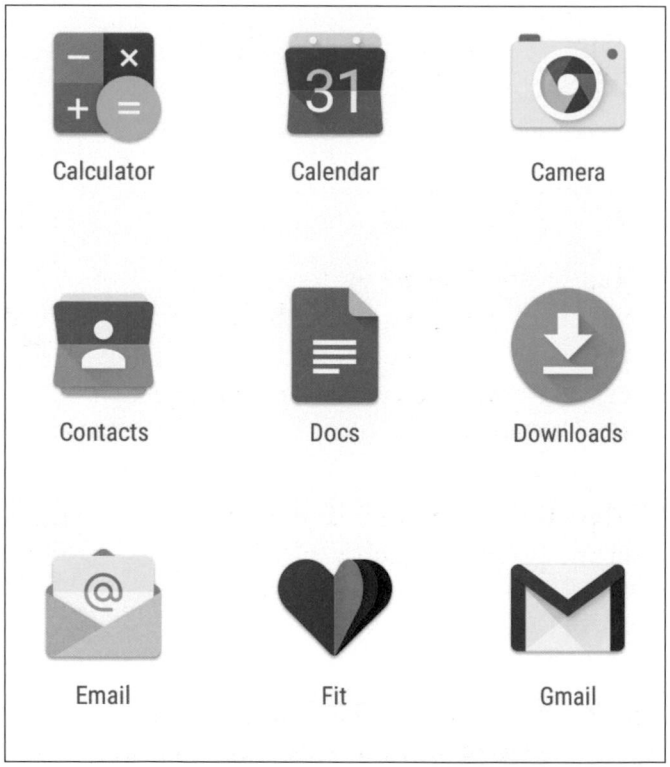

If your tablet is running low on memory it will automatically close any open apps to free up more memory. The ones that have been inactive for the longest period of time are the ones that are closed first, until enough memory has been freed up.

New apps for Android tablets are available through the Play Store, or directly from the developer's website. They can be downloaded from there and will then appear on your tablet.

Managing apps

Unless specified otherwise, Android apps are self-contained and do not interact with each other on your tablet. This has reduced the risk of viruses spreading through your tablet and also contributes to its memory management.

When you switch from one app to another you do not have to close down the original one that you were using. Android keeps it running in the background, but in a state of hibernation so that it is not using up any memory or processing power on your tablet. To do this:

For more information about the Navigation controls (including the Home button and Back button) see page 33.

1. Tap on an app to open it and move through its screens as required

2. Tap on the **Home** button on the tablet's Navigation bar at the bottom of the screen to return to the Home screen at any point. The app will remain open in the background

3. Tap on the app again. It will open up at the point at which you left it

You can also move back to the Home screen by tapping on the **Back** button. This takes you back through the screens that you have accessed within the app, until you reach the app's Home screen, at which point the next screen back will be the tablet's Home screen. If you do this, the next time that you access the app it will open at its own Home screen.

Makes and Models

Due to the open source nature of Android it can be used on a range of different devices and several manufacturers use it on their tablets. Two of the main Android tablets on the market are the Google Nexus, 9-inch version, and the Samsung Galaxy Tab 4, 7-, 8- and 10-inch versions.

Like most tablets, the Google Nexus has versions that can connect to mobile data networks, in the same way as a smartphone, using 3G or 4G services. These have to be paid for through the appropriate service provider and this will provide mobile Internet access even when you do not have Wi-Fi access.

Google Nexus 9

Google's flagship tablet, running the very latest version of Android, comes in a 9-inch version. The hardware is produced by HTC but it is very much a Google product and has excellent functionality in terms of processor speed, processor memory and storage.

Nexus controls

As with most tablets, the physical controls (On/Off, Volume) are located around the side of the Nexus (see page 26 for details). There are also various touchscreen controls that are located at the bottom of the screen:

1. Frequently-used apps can be pinned in the Favorites Tray, at the bottom of the screen, above the Navigation buttons

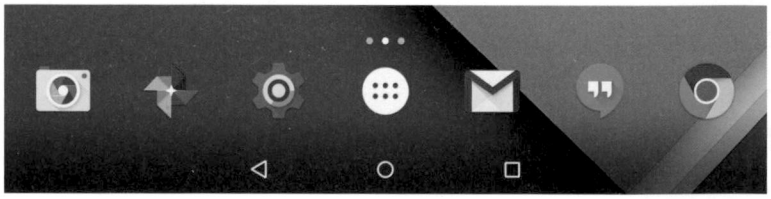

On some models of tablet, the All Apps button is located in the top right-hand corner of the screen.

2. Use this button to view All Apps

3. The dots above the All Apps button indicate how many Home screens are available. Tap on a dot to move to that Home screen (or swipe between them)

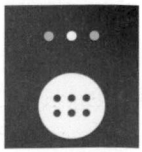

Samsung Galaxy Tab 4 (7-inch, 8-inch and 10-inch)

With its experience of using Android on its range of Galaxy smartphones, Samsung was well placed to enter the tablets market and it has done this successfully with its Tab 4 range of 7-inch, 8-inch and 10-inch tablets.

The main features are similar to those of the Google Nexus but, at the time of printing, it runs on a slightly earlier version of Android, 4.4 KitKat or earlier.

Samsung Tab 4 controls

The controls on the Samsung Tab 4 are similar to the Nexus, except that they are on the body of the device, rather than on the touchscreen, and they are, from left to right, the Recently-used app button, the Home screen button and the Back button.

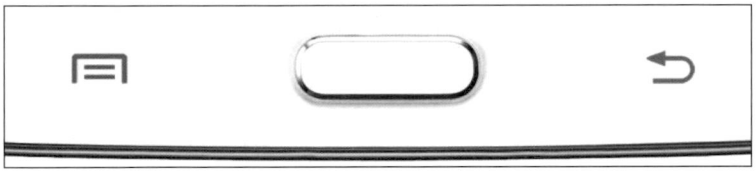

Samsung Note

This is similar in some respects to the Tab range, but much of its functionality is done with an S Pen, or stylus (see page 30).

Asus

This is an example of manufacturers developing hybrid tablets. In the case of the Transformer, this is done with a detachable keyboard/docking station.

Lenovo

This comes in 7-inch and 9-inch models and, in addition to apps from the Google Play Store, also provides access to apps in the Lenovo App Shop.

Sony Experia

This includes a range of 8-inch and 10-inch tablets that have high specifications, which are particularly good for gaming.

Samsung tablets have their own range of apps, in addition to the ones available from the Google Play Store. The Play Store apps for functions such as playing music and videos and reading books and magazines can be downloaded if they are not pre-installed on a Samsung tablet.

Android and Google

Most tablets are linked into a specific company for the provision of their services and selection of apps: Apple for the iPad, Amazon for the Kindle Fire and Google for tablets using Android. As with the other tablets, for Android ones you must have a linked account to get the most out of your tablet. This is a Google Account and is created, free of charge, with a Google email address (Gmail) and a password. Once it has been created it will give you access to a number of the built-in Android apps and also additional services such as backing up and storing your content.

If you already have a Gmail Account, this will also serve as your Google Account and the login details (email address and password) can be used for both.

When you first set up your tablet you can enter your Google Account details, or select to create a new account. You can also do this at any time by accessing one of the apps that requires access to a Google Account. These include:

- **Play Store**, for obtaining more apps.
- **Play Movies & TV**.
- **Play Books**.
- **Play Newsstand**.
- **Contacts**, for an online address book. When you enter contact details these are made available from any web-enabled device.

When you buy anything through your Google Account, such as music, apps or movies, you will have to enter your credit or debit card details and these will be used for future purchases through your Google Account.

When you access one of these apps you will be prompted to create a Google Account. You do not have to do so at this point, but it will give you access to the full range of Google Account services.

Other apps, such as the Photos app for storing and viewing photos, can be used on their own, but if a Google Account has been set up, the content will be backed up automatically.

Some of the benefits of a Google Account include:

- Access from any computer or mobile device with web access, from the page **accounts.google.com/** Once you have entered your account details you can access the **Dashboard** section, including your Calendar, Gmail and Play Store.

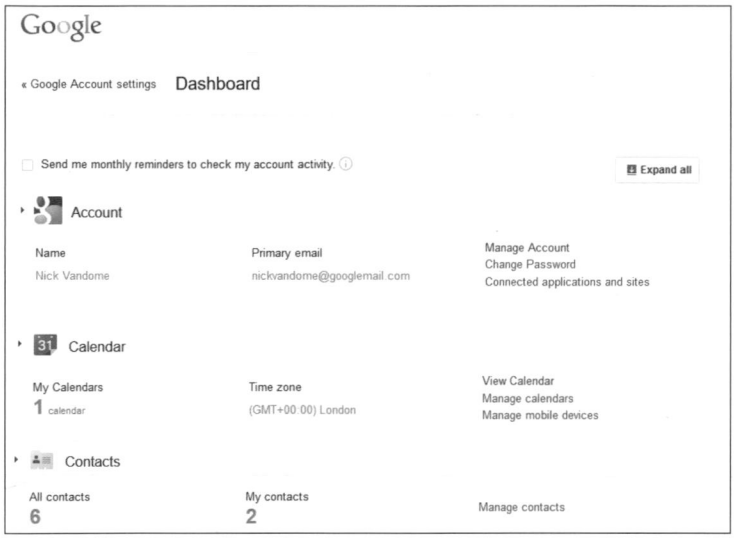

- Keep your content synchronized and backed up. With a Google Account, all of your linked data will be automatically synchronized so that it is available for all web-enabled devices and it will also be backed up by the Google servers.
- Peace of mind that your content is protected. There is a **Security** section on your Google Account web page where you can apply various security settings and alerts.

If you buy items from the Play Store through your Google Account on the Web, they will also be available on your Android tablet.

A new Google Account can also be created within **Settings > Accounts** on your tablet. Tap on the **Add account** button and tap on the **Google** button. Then enter the required details for the new Google Account (see pages 24-25).

Creating a Google Account

A new Google Account can be created in the following different ways:

- During the initial setup of your Android tablet.
- When you first access one of the relevant apps, as shown on page 22.
- From the **Settings** app and selecting the **Accounts** option.

For each of the above, the process for creating the Google Account is the same:

During the account setup process there is also a screen for account recovery, where you can add an answer to a question so that your account details can be retrieved by Google if you forget them.

1. On the **Add your account** screen, tap on the **Create a New Account** button

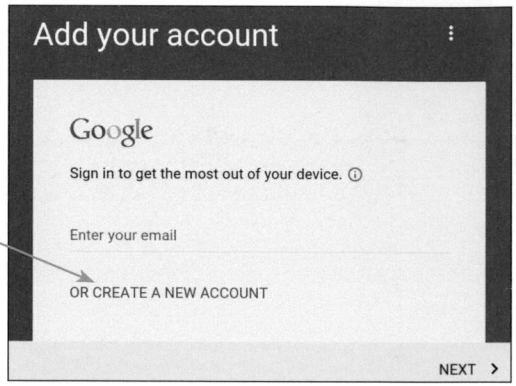

2. Enter the first and last name for the new account user and tap on the **Next** button

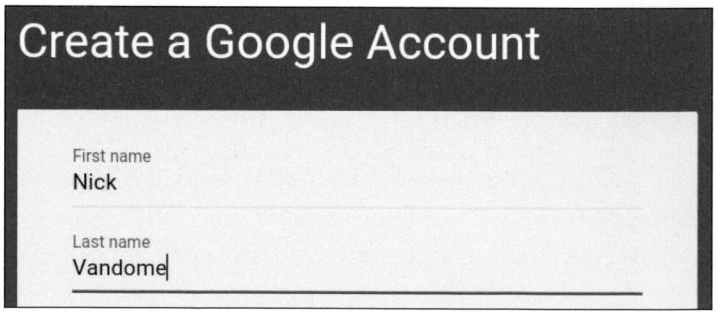

3. Enter a username (this will also become your Gmail address) and tap on the **Next** button at the bottom of the screen

4. Create a password for the account and then re-enter it for confirmation. Tap on the **Next** button at the bottom of the screen

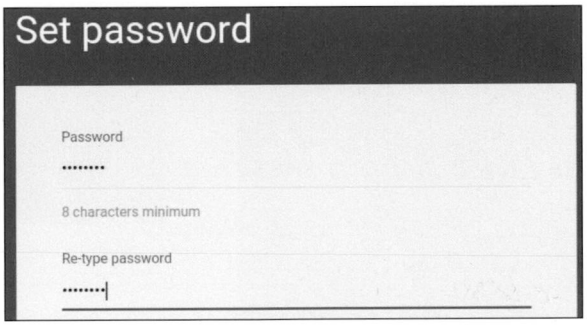

5. On the **Your Google Account** page, check on the required items and tap on the **Done** button

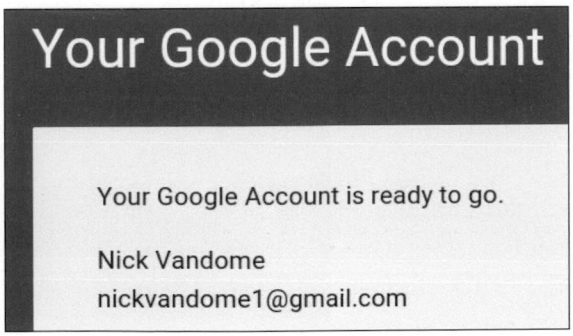

If your chosen username has already been taken you will be prompted to amend it. This can usually be done by adding a sequence of numbers to the end of it, but make sure you remember the sequence correctly.

Turning On and Controls

The button for turning a tablet on and off is located on the side of the body of the device in most cases, as are the other buttons and ports that can be used for various functions on your tablet.

Some tablets also have a slot for a SIM card, if they have the functionality for making phone calls through a mobile data provider.

On/Off button. This can also be used to put the tablet into Sleep mode. Press and hold for a couple of seconds to turn on the tablet. Press once to put it to sleep or wake it up from sleep.

Volume button. Press at the ends to increase or decrease volume.

Camera. This is the main, front-facing, camera for taking pictures.

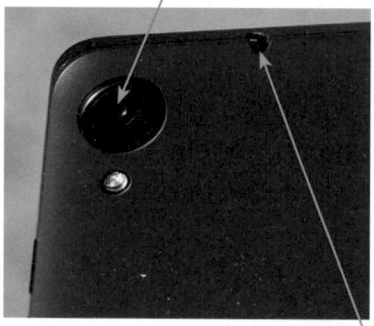

Headphone jack

The micro USB port on a tablet can be used to connect an HDMI cable, which can then be connected to an HD (High Definition) television so that you can view whatever is on your tablet on a large screen.

Micro USB port. This can be used to attach the tablet to an adapter for charging, or to a computer for charging or to download content from the tablet, using the supplied USB cable.

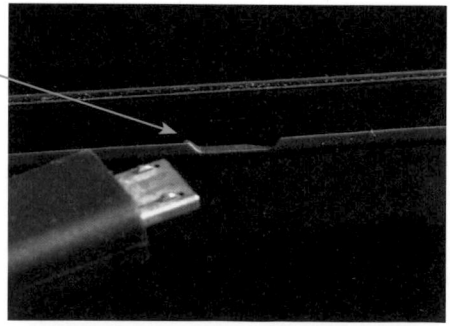

Most tablets have at least one camera; a front-facing one for video calls. Some also have a second camera, on the back, for taking photos and videos.

Battery and Charging

All tablets run on internal batteries which usually offer up to approximately 10 hours of average usage.

Tablet batteries can be charged with a USB adapter that connects via the tablet's micro USB port, with a supplied cable. This can also be connected to a desktop or laptop computer, but this takes longer to charge the tablet than using the dedicated adapter.

To charge a tablet's battery:

1. Attach the micro USB cable to the tablet

2. Connect the USB cable to the adapter, using the USB jack

3. Connect the adapter to the mains power. It is best to charge it fully before disconnecting it from the mains power, although it can still be used while it is being charged

To save battery consumption, turn down the screen brightness (**Settings > Device > Display**) and turn off Wi-Fi and Bluetooth if not in use (**Settings > Wi-Fi/Bluetooth**).

Setting Up Your Tablet

When you first turn on your tablet (by pressing and holding the On/Off button) you will be taken through the setup process. This only has to be done once and some of the steps can be completed, or amended, at a later time, usually within the **Settings** app. The elements that can be applied during the setup process are:

- **Language**. This option lets you select the language to use for your tablet. Whichever language is selected will affect all of the system text on the tablet and it will also apply to all user accounts on the tablet.

Most routers require a password when they are accessed for the first time by a new device. This is a security measure to ensure that other people cannot gain unauthorized access to your router and Wi-Fi.

- **Wi-Fi**. This can be used to set up your Wi-Fi so that you can access the Web and online services. In the **Select Wi-Fi** window, tap on the name of your router.

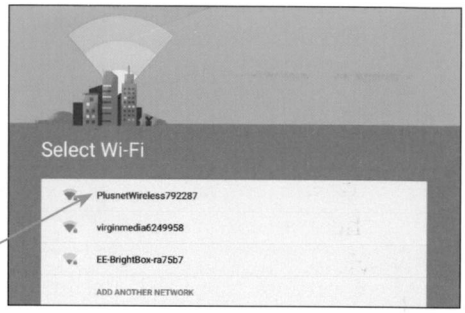

Enter the password for your router and tap on the **Connect** button.

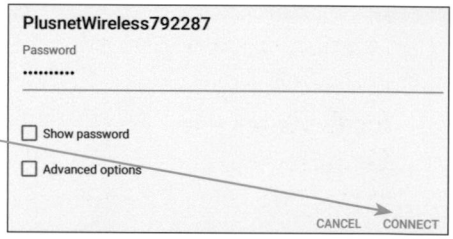

- **Google Account**. At this stage you can create a Google Account, or sign in with an existing one. Once you have done this you will have full access to the Google Account services and you will not have to enter your login details again.

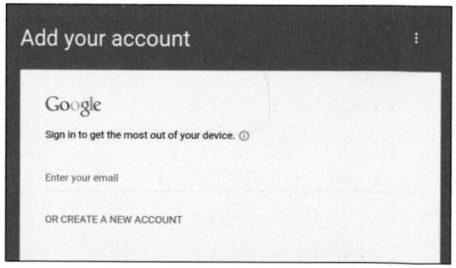

- **Apps & data**. This option can be used to set up your new tablet from a backup that you have made on another device. This will include all of the apps and settings that you have on the other device. You can also set up your tablet as a new device.

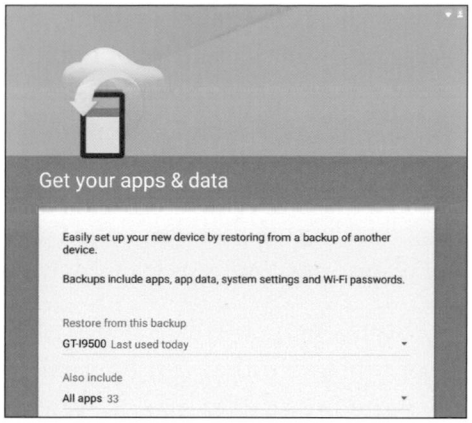

- **Google services**. This includes options for which of the Google services you want to use, including backing up your tablet, using location services and sending feedback to Google.

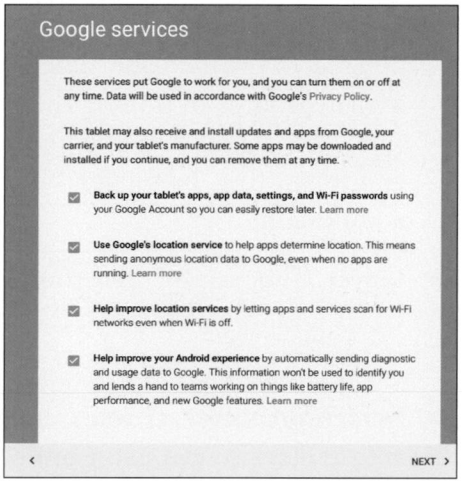

- **Google Now**. This is the personal digital assistant function that can be used to display a range of cards with the information that is most important to you (see pages 52-56).

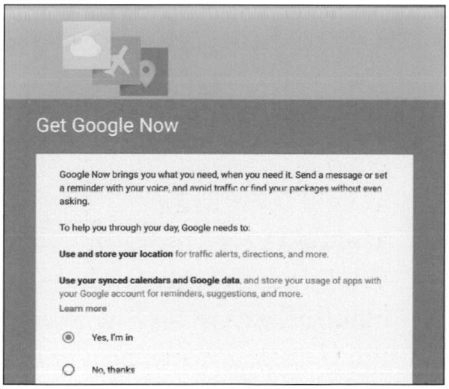

Adding Accessories

As with most electrical gadgets, there is a wide range of accessories that can be used with Android tablets. Some of these are more cosmetic, while others provide useful additional functionality. Some to consider are:

- **Docking station**. This can be used to attach to your tablet and it doubles as a stand for viewing content and also for charging your tablet.
- **Stylus pen**. This is a pen with a rubber tip that can be used to write on a tablet, tap on items to activate them and also swipe between screens or pages.

- **Battery charging pack**. This is a mobile unit that can be used to charge your tablet when you are away from a mains source of power. The pack is charged initially (indicator lights show how much charge is available) and it can then be plugged into the tablet to give it additional power.
- **Cover**. This can be used to protect the tablet and, in some cases, they double as a stand for viewing content on the tablet.

- **Screen protector**. If you want to give your tablet's screen extra protection, these sheets of clear plastic are a good option. Some of them also come with cleaning cloths.
- **USB adapter**. This is an adapter that connects to your tablet's micro USB connector so that USB devices can be connected to it. This can include digital cameras, pen drives and card readers for photos.
- **Mobile Wi-Fi unit**. This is a unit that can provide Wi-Fi access when you are away from your own Wi-Fi router. They are used with pay-as-you-go SIM cards so you only pay for what you use and do not need to have a long-term contract.

When you are buying accessories for your tablet, make sure that they are compatible with your device in terms of make and model.

Another useful accessory is a **Bluetooth keyboard**, which usually comes with a cover that acts as a stand for the tablet. It can be connected using the Bluetooth option in the Settings app.

2 Getting Started with Your Tablet

The interface for an Android tablet is more similar to that of a smartphone than a traditional computer. However, it also has many similar features to a computer and can perform a lot of the same tasks. This chapter details the Android interface and shows how to find your way around the Home screen, add apps and lock your tablet.

32 Viewing the Home Screen
33 Navigating Around
34 Adding Apps
35 Moving Apps
36 Working with Favorites
37 Adding Widgets
38 Changing the Background
39 Notifications
40 Creating Folders
41 Screen Rotation
42 Quick Settings
43 Accessing Settings
46 Locking Your Tablet
48 Searching
51 Ok Google
52 Using Google Now

Viewing the Home Screen

Once you have set up your tablet the first screen that you see will be the Home screen. This is also where you will return to when you tap the Home button (see next page).
The elements of the Home screen are:

There is also a **Quick Settings** area that can be accessed by swiping down from the top of the screen. See page 42 for more details.

Notifications Bar

Google Search box

Home screen area. This is where the majority of your commonly-used apps and widgets will be located

Favorites Tray

Navigation buttons

All Apps button

On different models of Android tablet, the Navigation buttons and All Apps button may be located in a slightly different position. The appearance of the Home screen may also be slightly different, depending on which apps the manufacturer wants to appear on the Home screen.

Navigating Around

At the bottom of the Home screen are three buttons that can be used to navigate around your tablet. These appear on all subsequent pages that you visit so that you can always use them for navigation purposes.

The Navigation buttons are:

Back. Tap on this button to go back to the most recently-visited page or screen.

Home. Tap on this button to go back to the most recently-viewed Home screen at any point.

Recent apps. Tap on this to view the apps that you have used most recently. Tap on one of the apps to access it again. Swipe an app to the right to close the app, or tap on the cross in the top right-hand corner of the app.

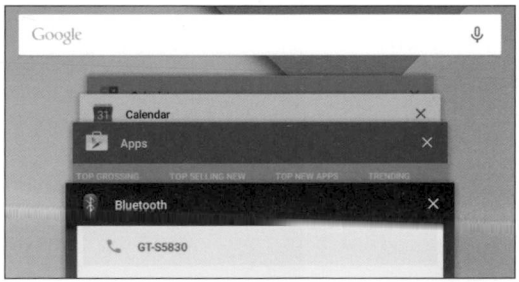

Going back

As well as using the Back button to return to the previous screen this can also be done, in some cases, via the icon for the relevant app at the top of the screen. For instance, if you are in the **Settings** app you can return to the previous screen by tapping on this button.

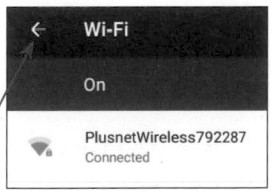

Most Android tablets have several Home screens. Swipe left and right to move between them.

When the keyboard is being used, the Back button turns into a down-pointing arrow. Tap on this once to hide the keyboard and reveal the Back button again.

Adding Apps

The Home screen is where you can add and manage your apps. To do this:

1. Tap on the **All Apps** button 

2. All of the built-in apps are displayed. Tap on an app to open it

3. To add an app to the Home screen, press and hold on it

4. Drag it onto the screen on which you want it to appear and release it

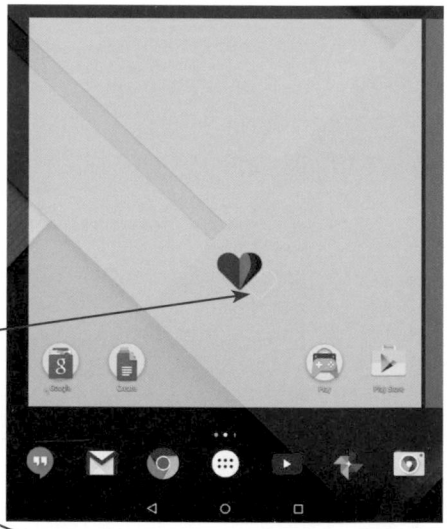

5. The app is added to the Home screen

6. Swipe left and right to move between the available Home screens

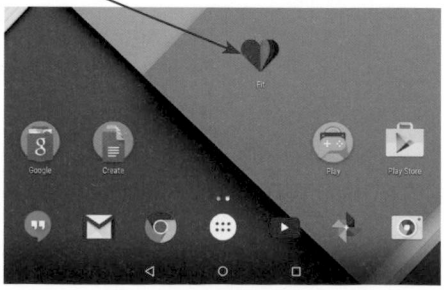

There are thousands more apps available for download from the Play Store. Tap on this button on the Home screen to access the Play Store.

Apps can be removed from a Home screen by dragging them to the top of the screen, where a **Remove** button will appear. Drag the app over the **Remove** button. This only removes it from the Home screen, not your tablet. It will still be available from the All Apps section.

Moving Apps

Once apps have been added to the Home screen they can be repositioned and moved to other Home screens. To do this:

1. Press and hold on an app to move it. Drag it into its new position. A light outline appears, indicating where the app will be positioned

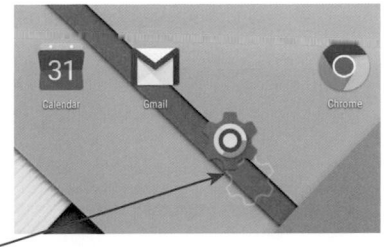

2. Release the app to drop it into its new position

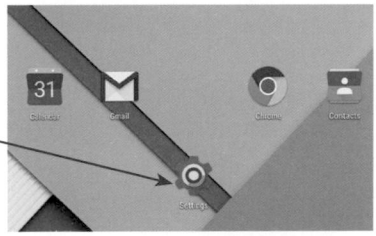

3. To move an app between Home screens, drag it to the edge of the Home screen

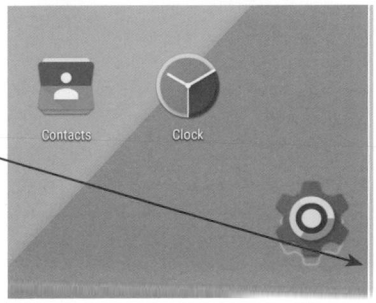

4. As the app reaches the edge of the Home screen it will automatically move to the next one. Add it to the new Home screen in the same way as in Step 2

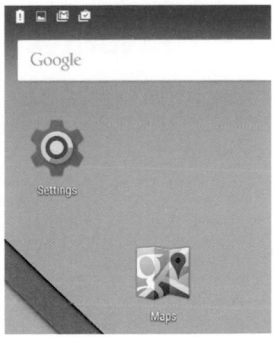

Apps can be moved to the left or right onto new Home screens.

Make sure that the app is fully at the edge of the Home screen, otherwise it will not move to the next one. A thin light border should appear just before it moves to the next Home screen.

Working with Favorites

The Favorites Tray at the bottom of the Home screen can be used to access the apps you use most frequently. This appears on all of the Home screens. Apps can be added to, or removed from, the Favorites Tray, as required.

For some tablets, the Favorites Tray appears along the bottom of the screen in landscape mode; for others, it appears down the right-hand side of the screen.

1. Press and hold on an app in the **Favorites Tray** and drag it onto the Home screen.
A gap appears where the app has been removed

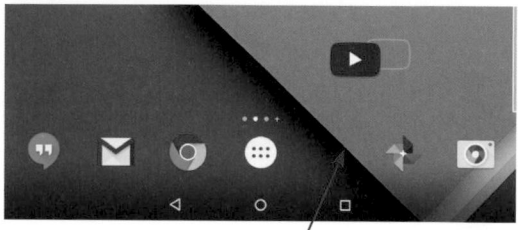

2. Tap and hold on the apps in the **Favorites Tray** and drag them into new positions as required

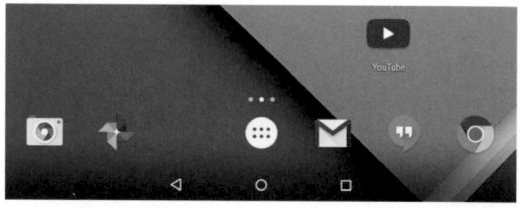

3. Press and hold on an app and drag it onto a space in the **Favorites Tray** to add it there

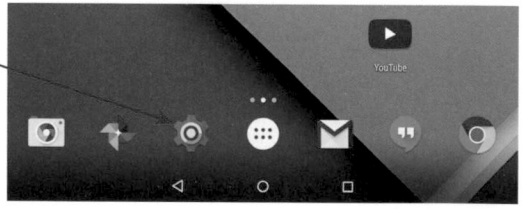

4. The **Favorites Tray** has a limit to the number of apps that it can contain (usually six) and if you try to add more than this the app will spring back to its original location

Apps can appear in the **Favorites Tray** and also on individual Home screens, but they have to be added there each time from within the **All Apps** section.

Adding Widgets

Android widgets are similar to apps, except that they generally display specific content or real-time information. For instance, a photo gallery widget can be used to display photos directly on a Home screen or a traffic widget can display updated information about traveling conditions. Widgets can be added from any Home screen:

1. Press and hold on an empty area on any Home screen and tap on the **Widgets** button

2. Swipe left and right to view all of the available widgets

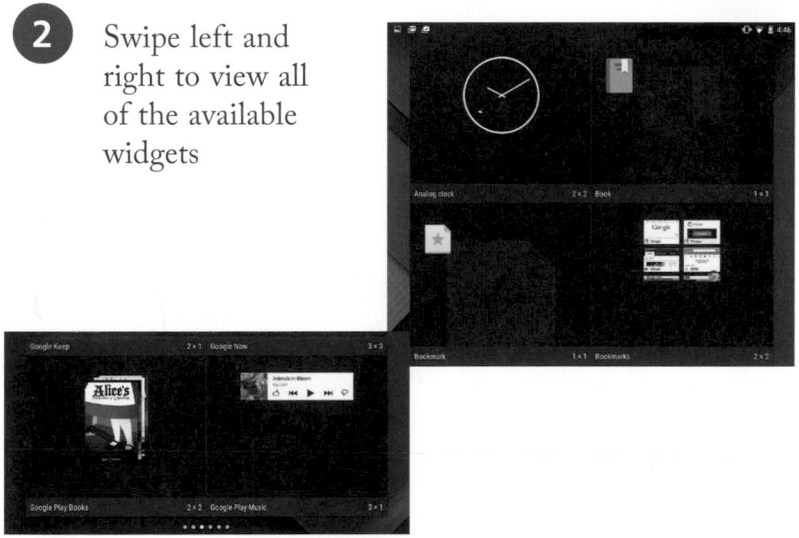

3. Press and hold on a widget and drop it onto a Home screen as required, in the same way as for adding apps

Widget icons on the Home screen usually appear larger than those for standard apps

Changing the Background

The background (wallpaper) for all of the Home screens on your tablet can be changed within the **Settings** app (**Settings > Wallpaper**). However, it can also be changed directly from any Home screen. To do this:

1. Press and hold on an empty area on any Home screen and tap on the **Wallpapers** button

2. Tap on one of the options from where you would like to select the background wallpaper

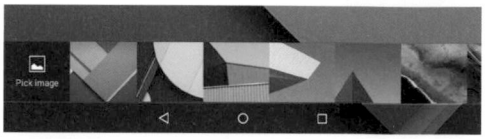

3. Swipe left and right to select a background

4. Select a background and tap on the **Set wallpaper** button

5. The selected background is applied to all Home screens

Wallpaper apps can be downloaded from the Play Store, to add a wider range of backgrounds to your tablet. Enter '**wallpaper**' into the Search box of the **Apps** section of the Play Store.

Notifications

Android tablets have numerous ways of keeping you informed; from new emails and calendar events, to the latest information about apps that have been downloaded and installed. To make it easier to view these items, they are grouped together in the Notifications area. This appears on the Lock Screen and can also be accessed from any Home screen from the Notifications bar.

1. By default, notifications are shown on the Lock Screen. Tap on a notification here to access it directly

2. On any Home screen, notifications are indicated on the Notifications bar

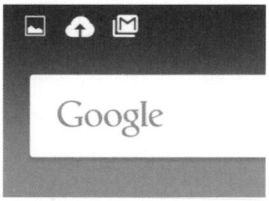

3. Swipe down from the top of any Home screen to access your notifications. Some of these may display more details than on the Lock Screen

4. Tap on a notification to view its full details, within the relevant app, e.g. open Gmail to view new emails

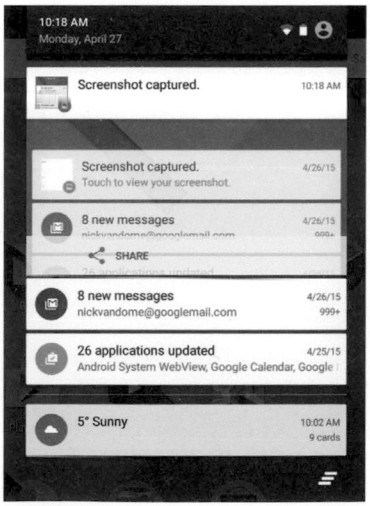

Settings for the Notifications area can be applied in **Settings > Sound & notification > Notification**. These can be used to specify what is shown when the tablet is locked and to select notifications for specific apps.

Tap on this button to clear all of the current notifications. If you clear the notifications it does not delete the items; they remain within their relevant apps and can be viewed there.

Creating Folders

As you start to use your Android tablet for more activities, you will probably acquire more and more apps. These will generally be for a range of tasks covering areas such as productivity, communications, music, photos, business and so on. Initially it may be easy to manage and access these apps, but as the number of them increases it may become harder to keep track of them all.

One way in which you can manage your apps is to create folders for apps covering similar subjects, e.g. one for productivity apps, one for entertainment apps, etc. To create folders for different apps:

To remove an app from a folder, press and hold on it and drag it out of the folder onto a Home screen.

1. Press and hold on an app and drag it over another one

2. Release the app. A folder will be created, containing both of the apps

3. Tap on a folder to view its contents. Initially it will be unnamed

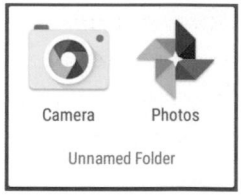

4. Tap here and give the folder a relevant name

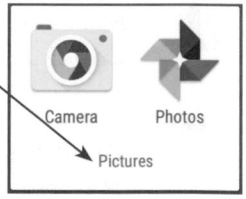

5. Folders can contain numerous items and also be placed in the **Favorites Tray**, in which case the folder name is not displayed

Adding folders to the Favorites Tray is a good way to make a larger number of apps available here, rather than the standard six permitted.

Screen Rotation

By default, the content on a tablet's screen rotates as you rotate the device. This means that the content can be viewed in portrait or landscape mode, depending on what is being used, e.g. for movies it may be preferable to have it in landscape mode, while for reading it may be better in portrait mode:

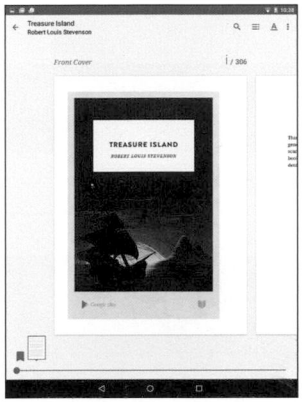

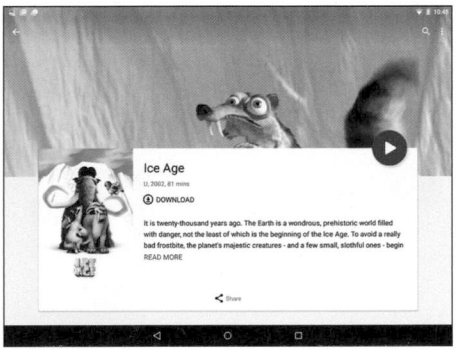

Screen rotation is achieved by a gyroscope sensor in the tablet.

It is also possible to lock the screen so that it does not rotate when you move it. This can be useful if you are using it for a specific task and do not want to be distracted by the screen rotating if you move your hand slightly. To lock and unlock the screen rotation:

1. Drag down twice from the top of the screen to access the **Quick Settings** (see page 42)

2. Tap on the **Auto-rotate** button to lock screen rotation

3. Tap on the **Portrait** button to disable the screen lock and return to Auto-rotate mode

Quick Settings

The full range of Android settings can be accessed from the Settings app. However, there is a Quick Settings option that can be accessed from the top of the screen. To use this:

1. Swipe down from the top of the screen to access the Notifications Area

2. Swipe down again on the top of the Notifications Area

3. All of the **Quick Settings** options are displayed

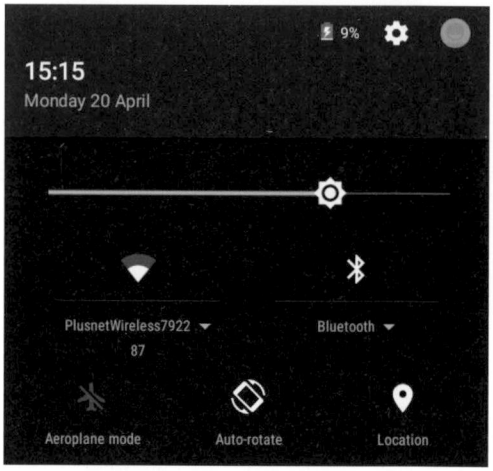

The Quick Settings can be accessed if the tablet is locked, but only with the Swipe method (see page 46 for details).

4. Tap on a setting to access its options in the **Settings** app, or

5. Tap on an item to apply it directly within **Quick Settings.** This can be done with **Aeroplane Mode**, **Auto-rotate** and **Brightness**. The **Brightness** option activates a separate widget that can be used to set the screen brightness

Accessing Settings

We all like to think of ourselves as individuals and this extends to the appearance and operation of our electronic gadgets. An Android tablet offers a range of settings so that you can set it up exactly the way that you want and give it your own look and feel. These are available from the **Settings** app.

To access the **Settings** on your Android tablet:

1. Tap on the **All Apps** button 
2. Tap on the **Settings** app 

3. The full range of settings is displayed

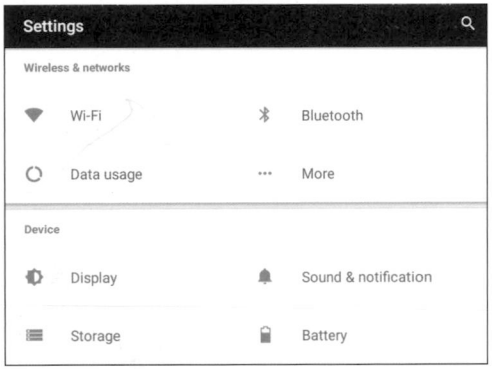

4. Tap on an item to view all of the options for it (if necessary, tap on the options at the next level down to see their own options). Most options will have an On/Off button, a radio button or a checkbox to tap on or off

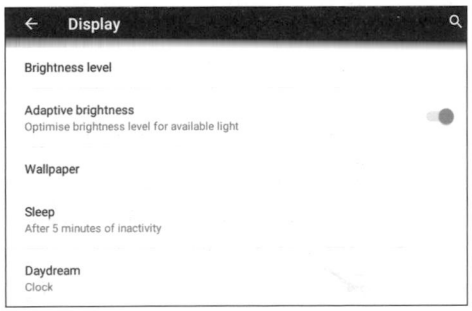

Add the **Settings** app to the **Favorites Tray** so that it is always quickly available.

Some settings may differ slightly between manufacturers but they will be broadly similar to those here. The settings shown here are for Android 5.0.

A radio button is round and appears with a dot inside it when it is selected; a checkbox is square and appears with a tick inside it when it is selected.

...cont'd

Wireless & Network

The Wireless & Network settings can be used to specify how you connect to the Internet and available wireless networks. The settings are:

- **Wi-Fi**. Used for turning Wi-Fi on and off on your tablet and connecting to a router.
- **Bluetooth**. Used for connecting wirelessly to other Bluetooth-enabled devices over short distances.
- **Data usage**. Used to view how much data you have downloaded.
- **Aeroplane mode**. Check this on when taking a flight.
- **VPN**. This stands for Virtual Private Network and is used to connect to a secure office network. Usually used to connect to a corporate network.
- **NFC**. Used to swap content between compatible devices by touching them back-to-back.
- **Android Beam**. Used together with NFC to transfer content, such as photos.

NFC stands for Near Field Communication and is a set of standards used for devices whereby they can communicate with each other using radio waves once they are touched together.

Device

The Device settings can be used to change the settings on your tablet for system sounds, display brightness, storage, battery usage, apps and individual users. The settings are:

- **Display**. Used to set the screen brightness, wallpaper and screen saver (Daydream).
- **Sound & notification**. This can be used to turn on or off the sounds used for the touchscreen, the Lock screen and docking.
- **Storage**. Shows what is using up the storage space on the tablet and how much is being used.
- **Battery**. Shows what is using up the battery power.

Daydream is a screen saver function that can be activated when the tablet is either charging or docked.

- **Apps (or Application Manager)**. Used to show information about the installed apps on the tablet.
- **Users**. Used to show the users and add more as needed.

Personal

The Personal settings can be used to specify how the information on your tablet is shared, security settings, language and input options and settings for how your content is backed up. The settings are:

- **Location (or Location Services)**. Used to specify whether apps can use GPS and Wi-Fi on your tablet to identify its location.
- **Security**. A range of security settings, for locking the tablet, encrypting its content and password details.
- **Accounts**. The Account settings can be used to add both Google and other accounts to your tablet.
- **Language & input**. Used to specify the system language for the tablet and also spelling and dictionary options.
- **Backup & reset**. Used for settings for backing up the data on your tablet and restoring it if required.

System

The System settings are used to set your preferences for your tablet. These include:

- **Date & time**. Used to set your tablet's date and time.
- **Accessibility**. Settings that can be used for users with visual or motor difficulties.
- **Printing**. Settings for saving compatible documents to the Google Drive (an online cloud storage service) so that they can be printed from there.
- **About tablet (or About device)**. This displays details about your tablet.

The **About tablet (or About device)** option under **System** displays the version of Android that is on your tablet.

Locking Your Tablet

Security is an important issue for any computing device and this applies to physical security as much as online security. For Android tablets it is possible to place a digital lock on the screen so that only an authorized user can open it. This is useful when there are several user accounts on the same tablet. There are different ways in which a lock can be set.

1. Tap on the **Settings** app

2. In the **Personal** section, tap on the **Security** button

3. The current method of **Screen lock** is displayed here. Tap on this to access the options

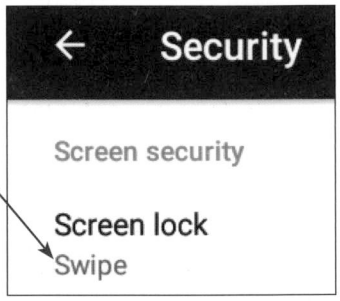

4. The methods for locking the screen are **Swipe**, **Pattern**, **PIN** and **Password**. Tap on the required method to select it and set its attributes

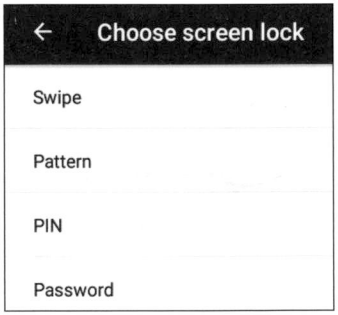

5. The **Swipe** option is the least secure as it only requires the padlock icon to be swiped to the edge of the circle to unlock the tablet. No other security authorization is required

The Swipe option is only really useful for avoiding items being activated accidentally when your tablet is not in use; it is not a valid security method. The most secure method is a password containing letters, numbers and characters.

6 For the **PIN** (or **Password**) option, enter the PIN in the box and tap on the **Continue** button. Enter the PIN again for confirmation. This will then need to be entered whenever you want to unlock the tablet

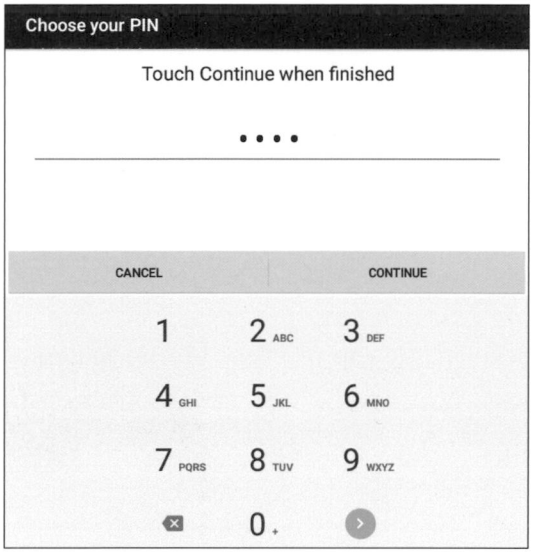

7 For the **Pattern** option, drag over the keypad to create the desired pattern

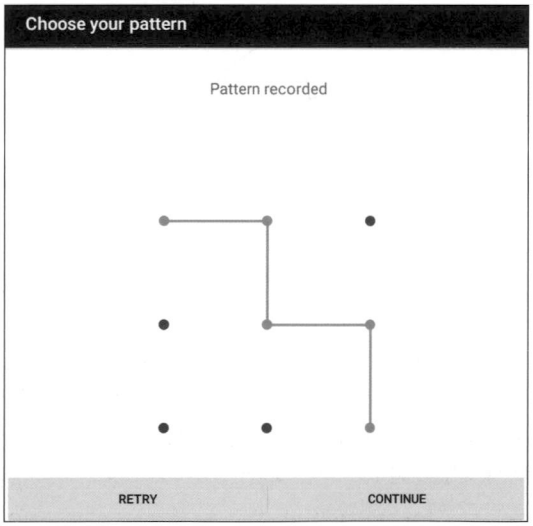

Whenever your tablet goes to sleep it will need to be unlocked before you can use it again. Sleep mode can be activated by pressing the **On/Off** button once. After a period of inactivity it will go into Sleep mode automatically: the length of time until this happens can be specified within **Settings > Display > Sleep**.

Searching

Since Android is owned by Google, it is unsurprising that tablets with this operating system come with the power of Google's search functionality. Items can be searched for on the tablet itself, or on the Web. This can be done by typing in the Google Search box and also by using the voice search option. To search for items on an Android tablet:

The Google Search box can also be accessed by swiping up from the bottom of the screen, from any app. This also displays the Google Now service, if it has been activated on your tablet.

1. By default, in portrait and landscape mode, the Google Search box appears at the top of every Home screen

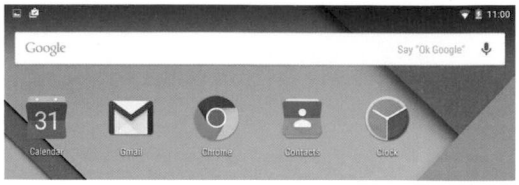

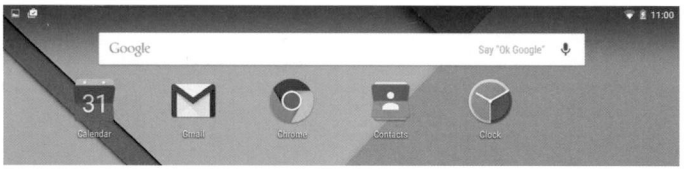

On some tablets, the search option is indicated by a magnifying glass with the word Google next to it.

2. Begin typing a word or phrase. As you type, corresponding suggestions will appear, both for on the Web and for apps on the tablet

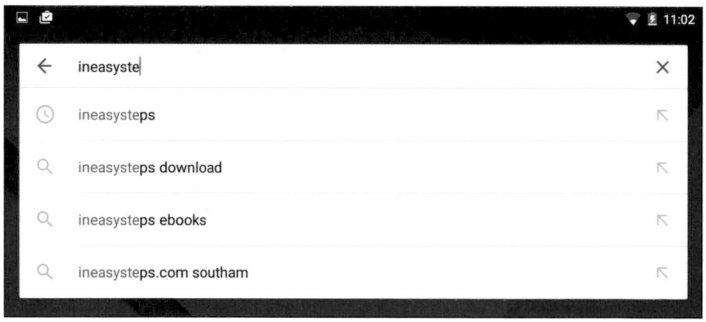

3. As you continue to type, the suggestions will become more defined

4. Tap on an app result to open it directly on your tablet, or tap on this button on the keyboard to view the results from the Web

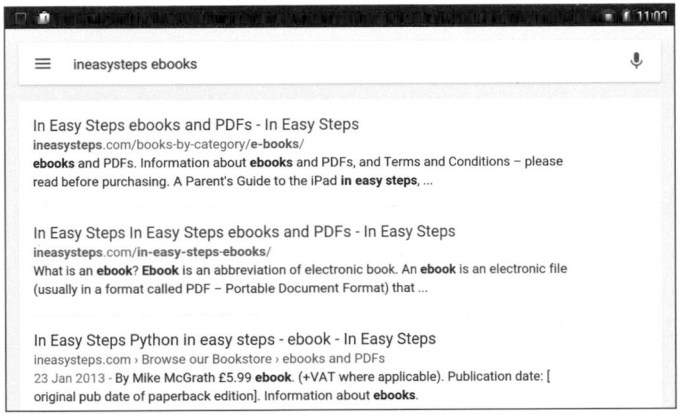

Voice search

To use the voice search functionality on your tablet, instead of typing a search query:

1. Tap on the microphone button in the Search box

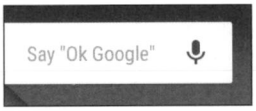

2. When the microphone button turns red, speak the word or phrase for which you want to search

The voice search functionality can also be used for items such as finding directions, setting alarms and finding photos on your tablet.

...cont'd

3. You can use voice search to find or open items on your tablet or from the Web. On your tablet you can use voice search to open apps, such as your Gmail app

4. The app opens in the same way as if you have tapped on it from the Home screen

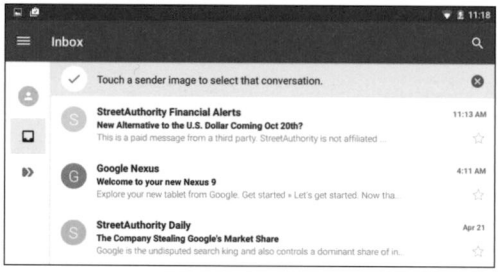

5. If you search for items on the Web, Google will use your location and also your search history to give you more accurate results, for instance if you search for 'Indian restaurants' it will display the results for those closest to your location

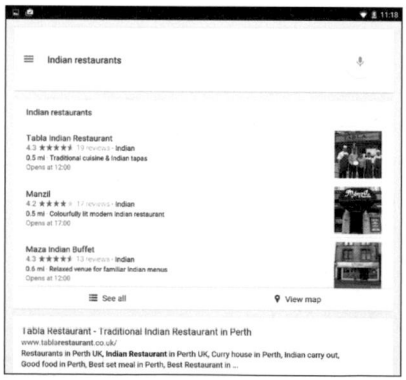

The phrase displayed in the voice search window is sometimes a summary of what you actually say. For instance, if you say, **'Please open Gmail app'**, the words **'open gmail'** may be displayed.

Ok Google

The latest version of Google Search on Android has a voice search function that can be activated by saying 'Ok Google' from any screen. You can then speak your search query as shown on the previous two pages. To use Ok Google:

1. Ensure you have the latest version of Google Search installed. This can be done from the Google Now screen or by selecting the Google Search app in the Play Store, to ensure it is up-to-date

2. Open the Google Search app and tap on the **Get Started** button

GET STARTED

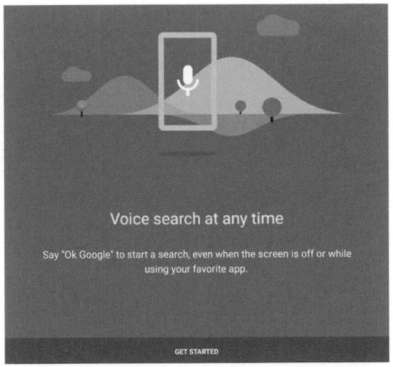

3. Train your tablet to recognize your voice by saying 'Ok Google' three times

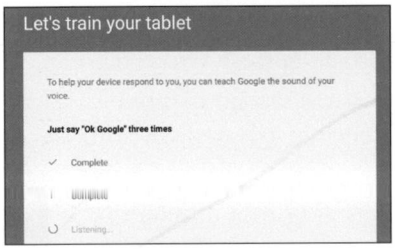

4. Tap on the **Finish** button to complete the setup for Ok Google. This can now be used from any screen on your tablet

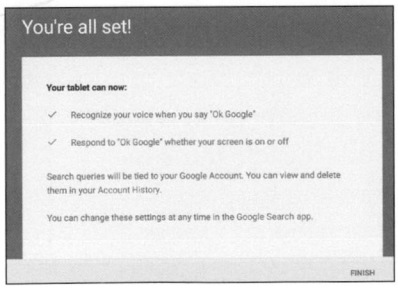

Using Google Now

We live in an age where we want the availability of as much up-to-date information as possible. On an Android tablet, one option for this is Google Now. This is a digital assistant service that provides items such as the latest traffic information for your area, flight information or the results from your favorite sports team. The information displayed is tailored to your needs according to your location and the type of content that you access.

When Google Now is activated this also turns on your location history so that Google can make use of the location data that is collected by your tablet.

To use Google Now on your tablet you have to be connected to the Internet via Wi-Fi.

Google Now cards

The functionality of Google Now is provided by cards. These display up-to-date information for a variety of topics. You can apply your own specific settings for each card and these will then display new information as it occurs. Cards appear when it is deemed that they are necessary, based on your location. So, if you are traveling in a different country, you will see a different range of cards from those when you are at home. Some of the most popular default cards include those for traveling to specific destinations (such as work) and sports cards.

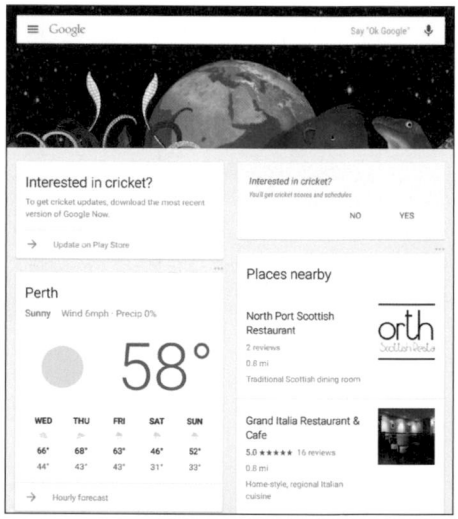

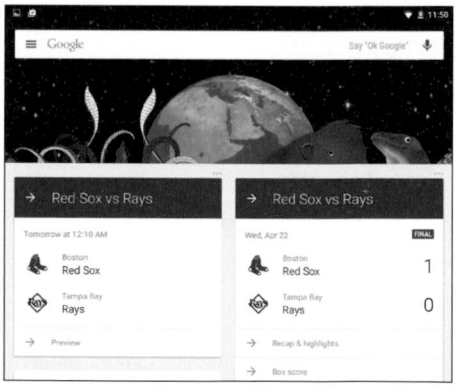

Google Now also accesses your web history, in order to provide you with as much relevant information as possible. This is stored as part of your Google Account and can be accessed by logging in with your account details at the website, **accounts.google.com** and accessing **Search History** under the **Dashboard** heading.

Accessing Google Now

By default, Google Now is not on (although it can be turned on during the initial setup process for your tablet). To activate it so that it works for you in the background:

1. Swipe up from the bottom of the screen
2. Tap on the **Get Google Now** button at the top of the screen

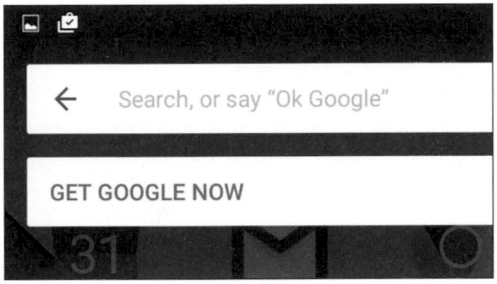

3. Tap on the **Yes, I'm In** button

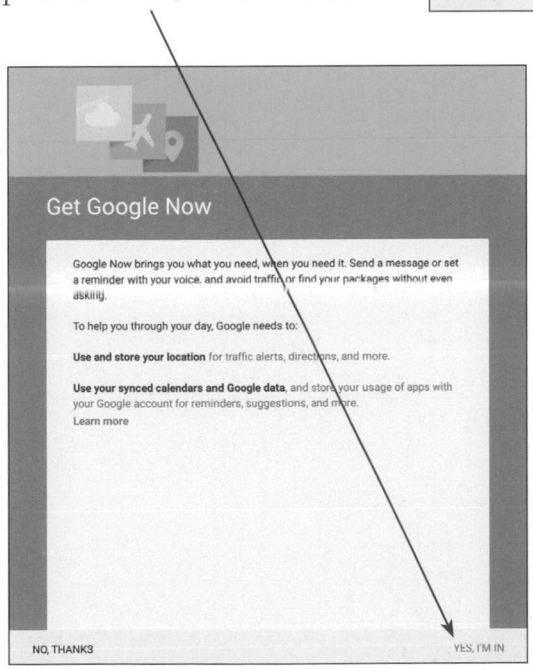

Google Now can also be accessed from the **Google** app in the **All Apps** section. Open this and continue from Step 3.

Some of the Google Now cards include: weather, traffic, sports, public transport, next appointment, news updates, stocks and travel. There is also a range of Gmail cards that can be used to track items that have been bought online and use Gmail for the confirmation email, such as packages, restaurant bookings and flights.

...cont'd

Around Google Now

When you first activate Google Now you will see the Home screen. This is where your cards will show up and from where you can access all of the settings for individual cards, such as selecting the way in which weather updates are displayed.

The Google Search box is located at the top of the Google Now Home screen. This can be used to search your Google Now cards, your tablet and also the Web.

1. Active cards are shown on the Home screen

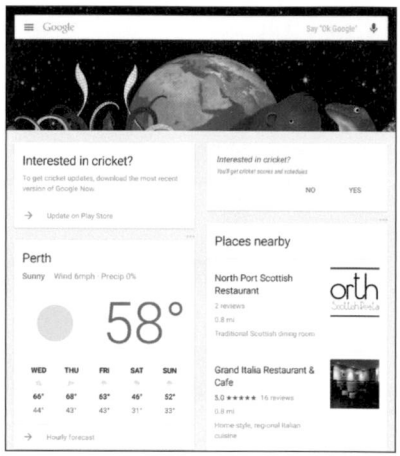

To delete a card, swipe it left or right off the screen. The card will come back the next time that the item is updated.

2. Tap here to view the card's individual settings

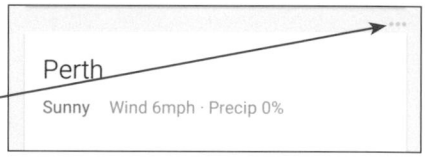

3. Specific settings can be applied for individual cards, such as the way in which the weather card displays its information

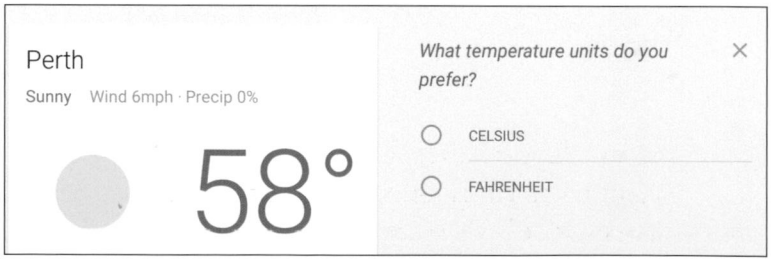

Customizing Google Now

Google Now can be customized so that you get exactly the type of information that you want. To do this:

1. Tap on this button at the top of the Google Now window

2. Tap on the **Customize** button

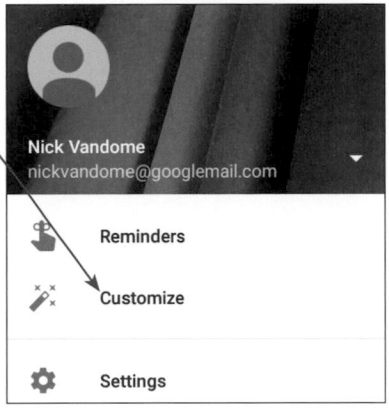

The **Settings** option in Step 2 provides a range of settings that can be applied for Google Search and also Google Now.

3. Tap on the items at the top of the window to specify the way in which directions are displayed

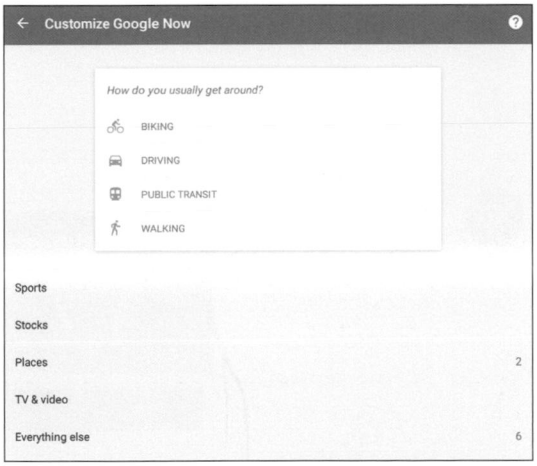

4. Tap on the categories at the bottom of the window to add more cards, including those for Sport, Stocks, Places and TV & video

...cont'd

5. For the items in Step 4, tap on a category and tap on an option to add another card, such as **Add a team**

6. Enter the name of the required item. For some options, suggestions will appear as you type

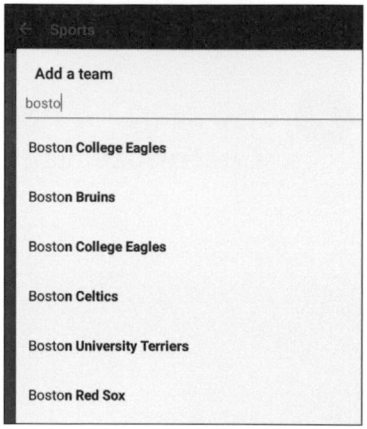

Only teams can be added from the Sports section on Google Now, not individual sportspeople.

7. The selected item is included as something in which you are interested

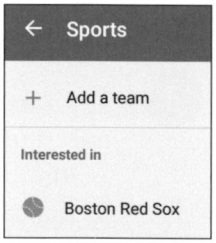

8. A card for the selected item is added to the Google Now Home screen. This can include items such as scores, reports and related videos

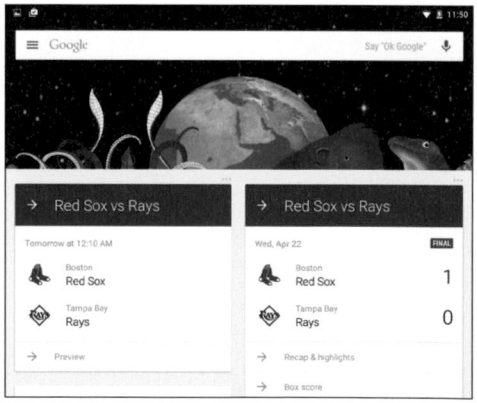

3 At Your Fingertips

This chapter introduces the touchscreen keyboard and shows how to add content with it.

58 The Android Keyboard

60 Keyboard Settings

62 Keyboard Shortcuts

64 Adding Text

65 Working with Text

66 Creating a Dictionary

The Android Keyboard

The keyboard on an Android tablet is a virtual one, i.e. it appears on the touchscreen whenever text or numbered input is required for an app. This can be for a variety of reasons:

- Entering text with a word processing app, email or an organizing app.
- Entering a web address.
- Entering information into a form.
- Entering a password.

The examples in this chapter are from the Google Nexus. The keyboards on other tablets may differ slightly.

Viewing the keyboard

When you attempt one of the items above, the keyboard appears before you can enter any text or numbers:

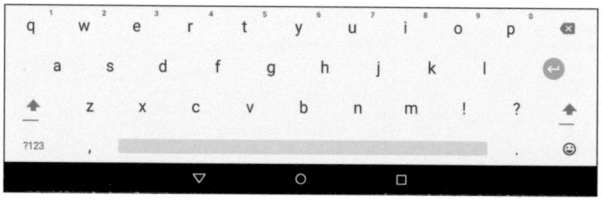

When using the keyboard, it only requires a light touch: you do not have to press very hard to activate the keys.

Around the keyboard

To access the various keyboard controls:

Additional keyboards can also be downloaded from the Play Store, if you want to try different ones from the default one.

1. Tap once on this button to add a single capital letter (the keyboard letters are displayed as capitals)

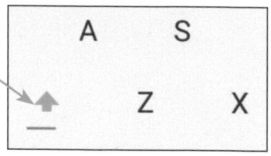

2. Double-tap on this button to create **Caps Lock**. This is indicated by a blue line underneath the arrow

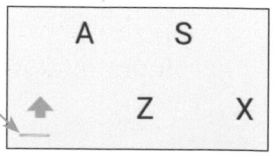

3. Tap on this button to back-delete an item

4 Tap once on this button to access the **Numbers** keyboard option

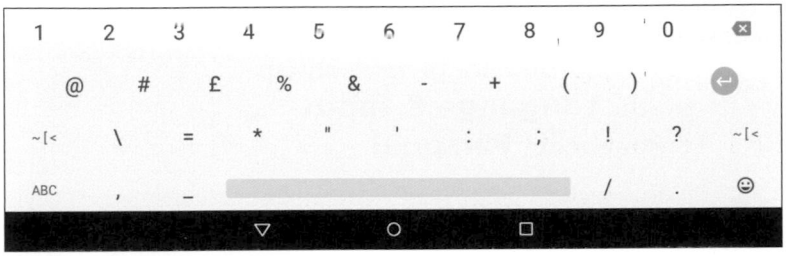

5 From the Numbers keyboard, tap once on this button to access the **Symbols** keyboard

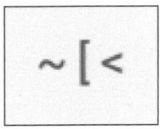

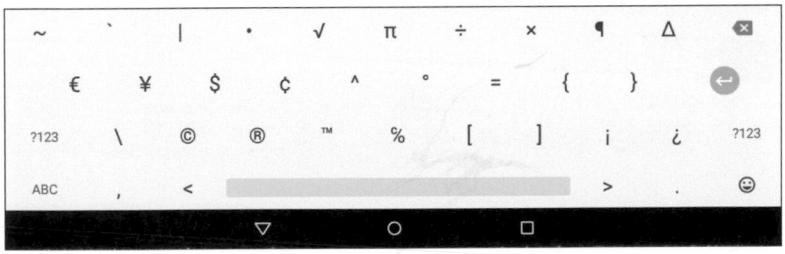

6 Tap once on this button on either of the two keyboards above to return to the standard **QWERTY** option

7 Tap once on this button to hide the keyboard (this can be done from the Navigation bar at the bottom of the screen). If the keyboard is hidden, tap once on one of the input options, e.g. entering text, to show it again

If you are entering a password, or details into a form, the keyboard will have a **Go** or **Send** button that can be used to activate the information that has been entered.

Keyboard Settings

There are a number of options for setting up the functionality of your Android tablet's keyboard. These can be accessed from the Personal Settings:

The Nexus used in this book has been set up for English (UK) – see page 28.

1. Open the **Settings** app and tap on the **Language & input** button under **Personal**

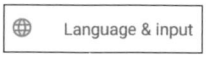

2. Tap here to enable the **Spell checker**

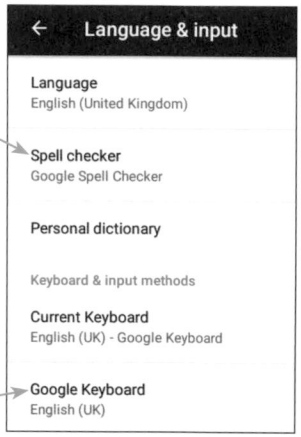

3. Tap here to access the settings for the default Google Keyboard

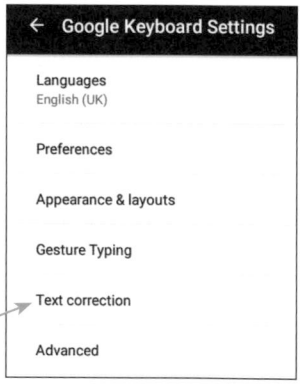

4. Tap on the **Text correction** button

5. Tap on the **Add-on dictionaries** button to add more dictionaries to the keyboard

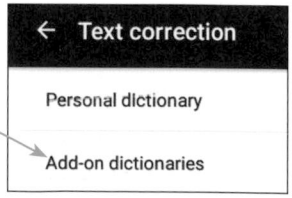

If the Spell checker is turned on, misspelled words will be underlined in red when they are entered with the keyboard.

6 Tap on the **Auto-correction** button under **Text correction**

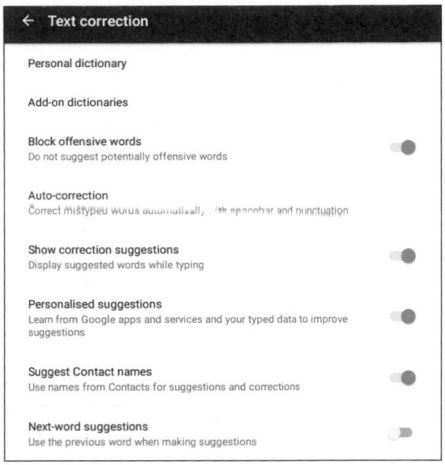

7 Tap on a radio button for the level of auto-correction

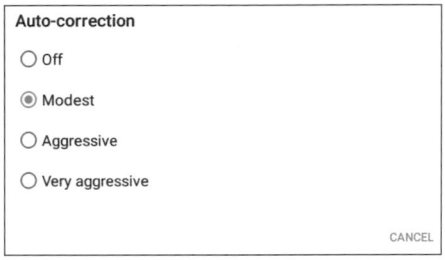

Tap the **Show correction suggestions** button On under **Text correction** to display suggested words as you type.

8 Tap the **Next-word suggestions** button On in Step 6 for auto-correction, which helps to make the suggestion in the context of what is being written

9 Tap on the **Advanced** button to access the advanced settings for the Google Keyboard, including sending usage statistics to Google

Advanced

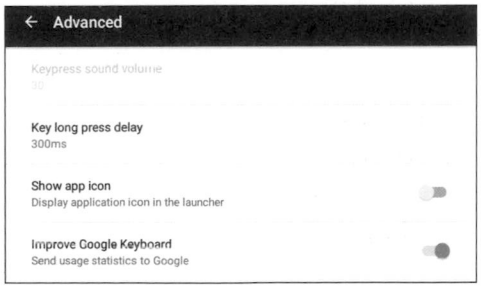

Keyboard Shortcuts

Because of the size of the keyboard on an Android tablet, some of the keys need to have duplicate functionality, in order to fit in all of the options. This includes keys with dual functions, accented letters and keyboard settings options.

Much of this functionality is accessed by pressing and holding on keys, rather than just tapping on them once.

Keyboard settings

To access the keyboard settings directly from the keyboard:

1. Press and hold on this button

2. Tap on the **Settings** button

3. Tap on **Input options > Languages** or **Google Keyboard Settings** to access the full range of settings for the keyboard

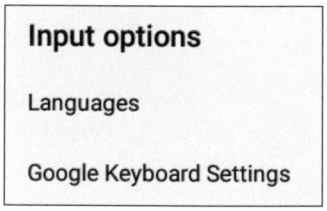

Some tablets may have their own keyboard settings, but they are similar to those for the Google Keyboard.

Dual functions

If a key has more than one character on it, both items can be accessed from the same button.

1. Tap on a button to insert the main character

2. Press and hold on the button to access the second character (in the top right-hand corner of the key). Release the button to insert the character

Accented letters

Specific letters on the keyboard can also be used to include accented letters for words in different languages.

1. Press and hold on a letter that has corresponding accented versions in different languages. Tap on a letter to insert it

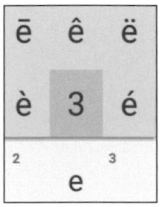

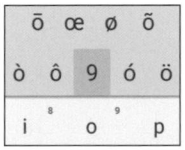

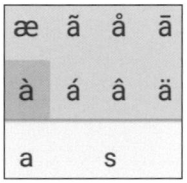

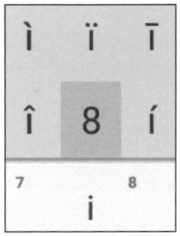

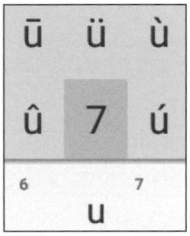

The accented letters are available on the keyboard regardless of which language dictionaries are installed.

2. The **Return** key also has a **Previous** button that can be accessed by pressing and holding on it. This can be used when filling in online forms

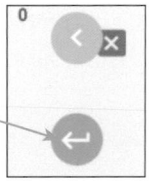

Numbers can be added from the Numbers keyboard and also by pressing and holding on the top line of the QWERTY keyboard and swiping over a number.

Spacebar shortcut

The spacebar can also be used for a useful shortcut at the end of a sentence, double-tap on the spacebar to add a full stop/period and a space, ready for the start of the next sentence. This can be specified within **Google Keyboard Settings > Preferences**.

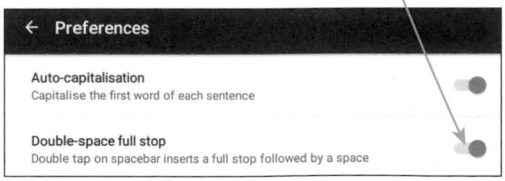

Adding Text

Once you have applied the keyboard settings that you require you can start entering text. To do this:

If you do not want to use the underlined auto-correction word, tap on one of the others on the bar above the keyboard. Tap on it again to save the word to your own custom dictionary, so that auto-correction will remember it the next time you want to use it.

1. Tap once on the screen to activate the keyboard. Start typing with the keyboard. The text will appear at the point where you tapped on the screen

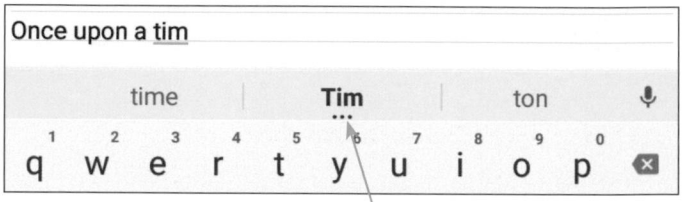

2. If **Auto-correction** is enabled, suggestions appear above the keyboard. Tap once on the spacebar to accept the suggestion with the dots underneath it, or tap on another word to insert that instead

3. If the **Spell checker** is enabled, any misspelled words appear underlined in red

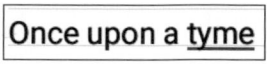

4. Tap on a misspelled word to view suggested alternatives. Tap on one to replace the misspelled word, or add it to the dictionary, or delete it

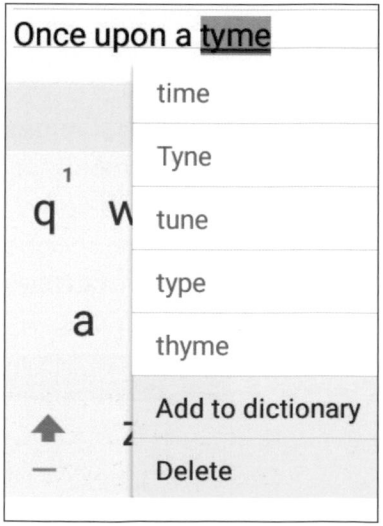

Tap on the right-hand word on the list above the keyboard to view additional suggestions.

Working with Text

Once text has been entered it can be selected, copied, cut and pasted, either within an app or between apps.

Selecting text

To select text and perform tasks on it:

1. Tap anywhere to set the insertion point for adding, or editing, text

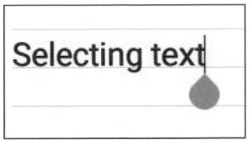

2. Drag the marker to move the insertion point

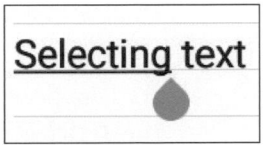

3. Double-tap on a word to activate the selection handles

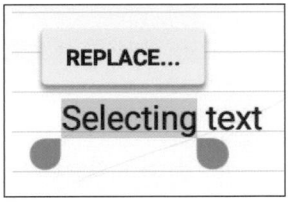

4. Drag the handles to change the text that is selected

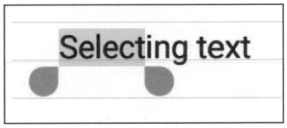

5. Tap on these buttons at the top of the window to **Cut** or **Copy** the selected text

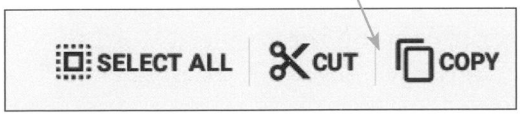

6. Locate the point at which you want to include the text. Press and hold and tap on **Paste** to add the text

There is usually a **Paste** option on the main toolbar of apps in which you want to paste text that has been copied.

Creating a Dictionary

In addition to the standard dictionaries on your Android tablet it is also possible to create your own custom dictionary. This could include real names, or words which you use regularly but do not appear in the virtual dictionary. To create your own dictionary:

Do not use a shortcut that is an actual word, otherwise it could cause confusion.

1. Access **Settings > Language & input > Google Keyboard > Text correction** and tap on the **Personal dictionary** button

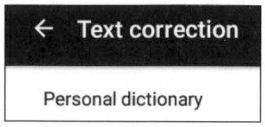

2. At this point the dictionary will be empty. Tap on the **Add** button to create an entry

3. Enter the word, or phrase, and a shortcut with which to enter it. Tap on this arrow on the keyboard

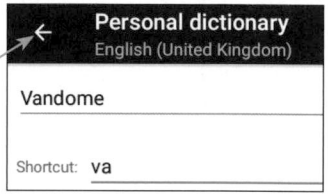

4. Tap on this button on the keyboard. The entry is added to your custom dictionary

5. When entering text, enter the shortcut. The word will appear on the options bar above the keyboard. Tap on the required word to insert it

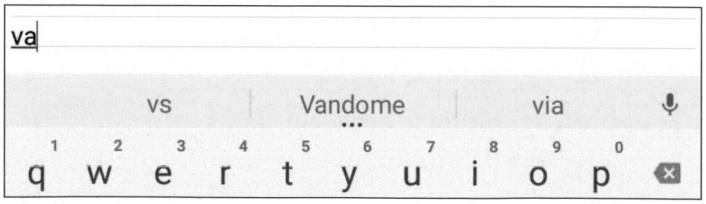

4 Working with Apps

Apps on an Android tablet are the programs that provide its functionality. This chapter details the built-in ones and shows how to obtain more.

68 About Android Apps
69 Built-in Apps
72 Around the Play Store
74 Finding Apps
76 Downloading Apps
78 Deleting Apps
79 Updating Apps
80 App Information

About Android Apps

An app is just a more modern name for a computer program. The terminology first became widely used on smartphones, but has now spread to all forms of computing and is firmly embedded in the language of tablets.

On Android tablets there are two types of apps:

- **Built-in apps**. These are the apps that come pre-installed on your Android tablet.
- **Play Store apps**. These are apps that can be downloaded from the online Play Store.

In addition to the Play Store, some tablet manufacturers also offer their own apps stores, although the range of apps is usually more limited.

Using apps

To use apps on an Android tablet:

1. The full range of Android apps can be viewed by tapping on the **All Apps** button

2. Tap once on an app to open it

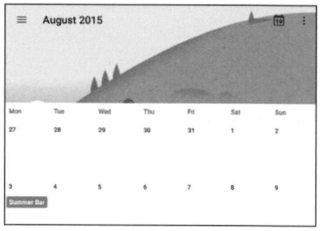

3. Tap on either of the **Menu** buttons to access individual settings for a specific app

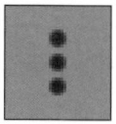

Built-in Apps

The built-in apps that are available from the All Apps screen can vary slightly depending on the brand of Android tablet being used. However, some of the generic apps should include:

- **Calculator**. A standard calculator that also has some scientific functions, although not the range of a full scientific calculator.

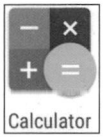

- **Calendar**. An app for storing appointments, important dates and other calendar information. It can be synced with your Google Account.

- **Chrome**. Different Android tablets have different types of browsers for accessing the Web. The Chrome browser is the default on some tablets.

- **Clock**. This can be used to view the time in different countries and also as an alarm clock and a stopwatch.

- **Contacts**. This is the Android address book where you can enter details about your friends and family members. It can also be synced with your Google Account.

- **Docs**. This can be used to create word processing documents and keep them in cloud storage (online storage) or on your tablet.

- **Downloads**. When you download content onto your tablet this can be viewed and managed in this app. It can also be used to view web pages offline.

- **Drive**. This is another Google app and provides online storage and backup for documents and files on your tablet.

Because of the open source nature of Android, manufacturers can customize the built-in apps for their devices. The apps here are for the Google Nexus.

...cont'd

- **Email**. Although this is still included with tablets, the Email app is now redundant as the Gmail app has taken over all email accounts.

- **Fit**. This is an app for monitoring and recording your fitness activities. You can set your own goals and check your progress against them.

- **Gmail**. When you set up a Google Account you will also create a Gmail account for sending and receiving email. This app can be used for accessing and using your Gmail.

- **Google**. This app can be used for accessing the Google Search function, still one of the best search facilities available. It can also be used for accessing the Google Now function, if set up.

- **Google+**. This can be used with your Google Account to share content such as photos and updates with specific people.

- **Google Settings**. This app can be used for specific Google settings on your tablet such as searching, giving access to your location and opting out of some advertisements.

- **Keep**. This is like an digital pinboard where you can add notes, reminders and lists.

- **Hangouts**. This is a Google social media app that can be used to chat with friends using either text or video and share photos.

- **Maps**. Google Maps app is one of the best mapping apps available for finding locations and obtaining directions.

The **Settings** app is also available in the All Apps section and it is a good idea to add this to the **Favorites Tray** for quick access from any Home screen. For more details about the Settings app see pages 43-45.

- **Photos**. This is the default Android app for viewing, managing and sharing your photos.

- **Play Books**. This is the app for reading ebooks on an Android tablet. It can be used to manage books in your library and also download new ones from the Play Store.

- **Play Games**. This is the app for accessing games from the Play Store and playing them on your tablet.

- **Play Movies & TV**. Another app linked to the Play Store. It is used to view movies that you have bought or rented from the Play Store and to view your own personal videos.

- **Play Music**. This is the default music player that can be used to play your own music and also music content from the Play Store.

- **Play Newsstand**. Similar to the Play Books app, this is used for reading magazines and downloading new ones from the Play Store.

- **Play Store**. This is where all of the online content for Android tablets can be accessed, bought and downloaded. This includes apps, books, music, movies and magazines.

- **Sheets**. This can be used to create spreadsheets and keep them in cloud storage (online storage) or on your tablet.

- **Slides**. This can be used to create presentations and keep them in cloud storage (online storage) or on your tablet.

- **YouTube**. This provides direct access to the popular video sharing website.

Some Android tablets have different apps for functions such as playing music and movies and reading books and magazines. If this is the case, the Play ones here can still be downloaded from the Play Store.

Around the Play Store

Although the built-in apps provide a lot of useful functionality and are a good starting point, the Play Store is where you can really start to take advantage of the wide range of apps that are available. These can be used for entertainment, communication, productivity and much more.

To access the Play Store and find apps:

New apps are added to the Play Store on a regular basis (and existing ones are updated) so the Homepage will change appearance regularly.

1. Tap on the **Play Store** app 
2. Suggested items are shown on the Play Store Homepage

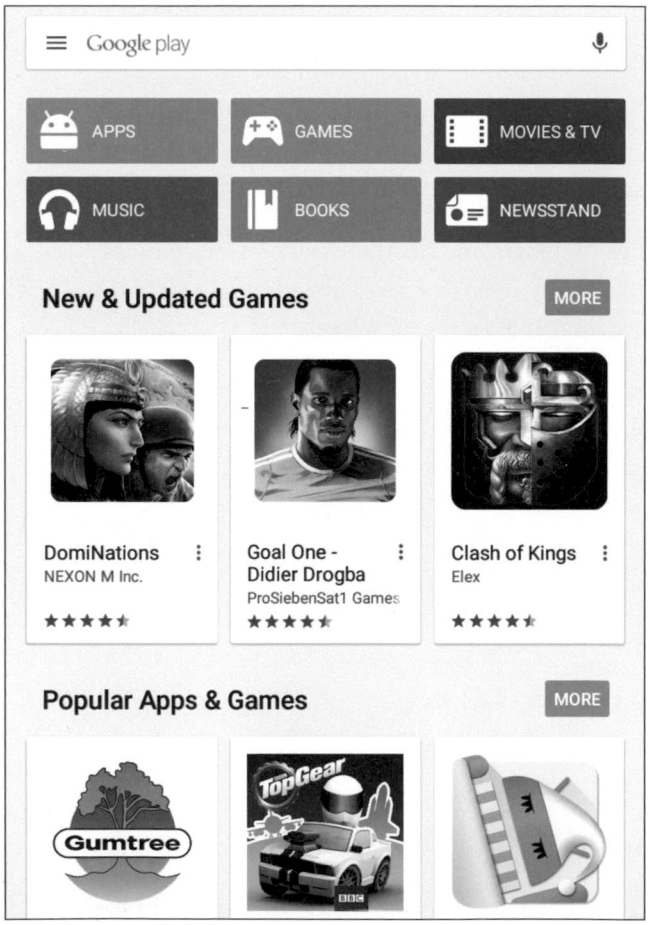

App prices are shown in the local currency.

3 Swipe up and down to see the full range of recommendations, for all types of content in the Play Store. Tap on an item to view further details about it

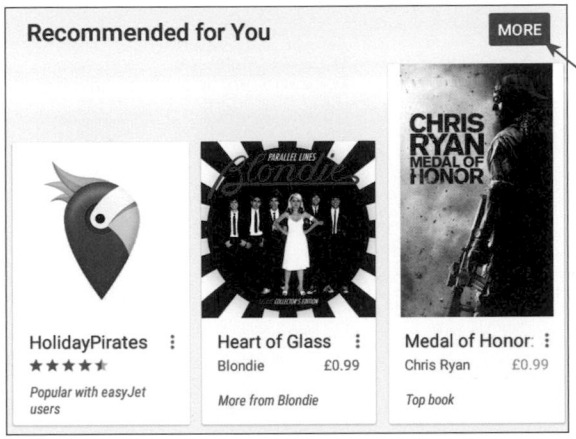

Tap on the **More** button in a section on the Homepage to view additional items.

MORE

4 Use these buttons to find content according to specific categories. Tap on the **Apps** button to view the range of apps in the Play Store

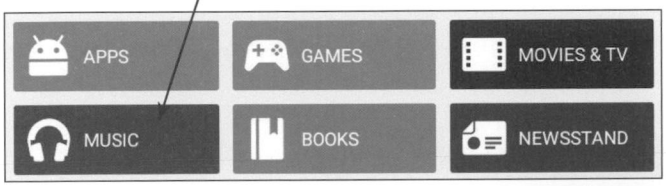

5 Tap on the **Menu** button to access the Play Store menu

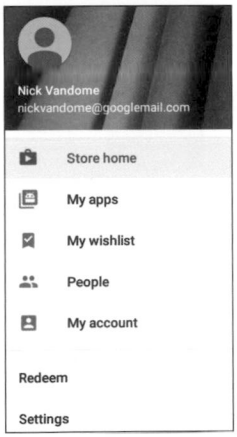

If you have a Play Store Gift Card, it can be redeemed from the **Redeem** button which can be accessed from the Menu button at the top of the Play Store window. Enter the Gift Card code and the relevant amount will be credited to your Google Play balance for use in the Play Store.

Finding Apps

Searching by category

When you have accessed the Apps section of the Play Store you can then look for content in a variety of ways:

1. The featured and recommended items are displayed on the Apps Homepage. Swipe up and down to view the full range and tap on an item to view more details

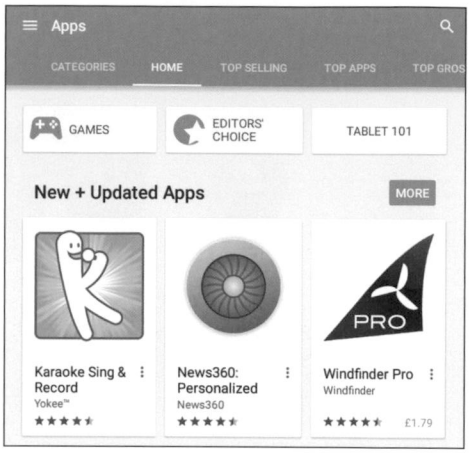

There may be different apps available in the Play Store depending on your geographical location.

2. Swipe left and right on the top bar to view apps according to Categories, Home, Top Selling, Top Apps, Top Grossing, Top Selling New, Top New Apps and Trending

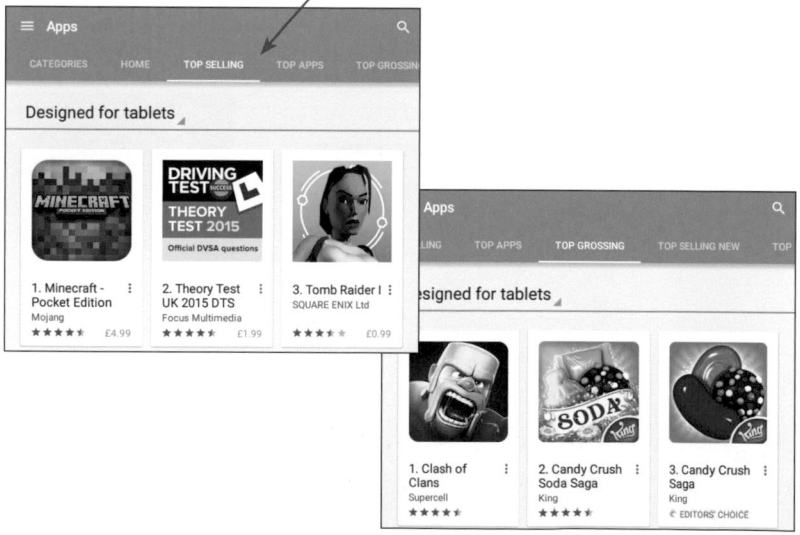

3. Tap on the **Categories** tab and tap on a category to view the apps according to these headings

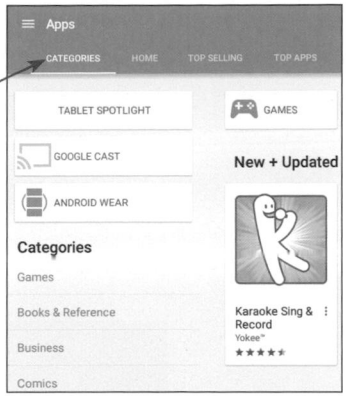

4. Search for apps within a category in the same way as for searching over the whole range of apps as in Step 2

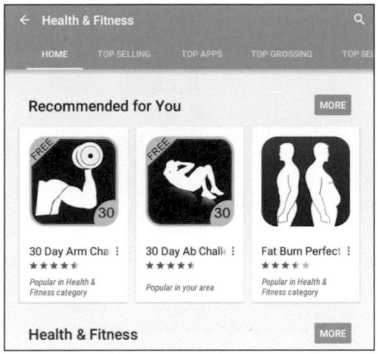

Using the Search box

1. Tap on this button to search for specific items

2. Enter the name of the item for which you want to search

3. Tap on one of the suggested results or tap on this button on the keyboard

Downloading Apps

Once you have found an app in the Play Store that you want to use, you can download it to your tablet:

1. Access the app you want to use. Tap here to view a video preview of the app (if available). There will also be details about the app and reviews from other users

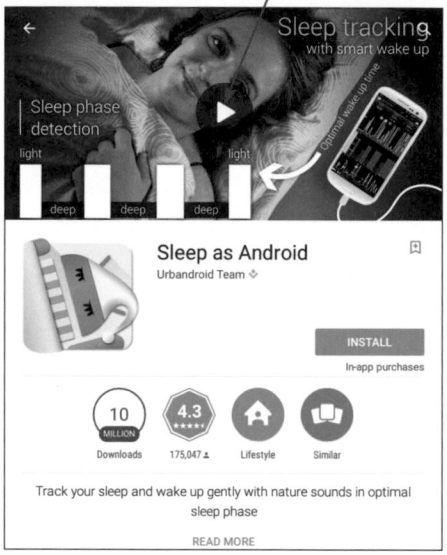

2. Tap on the **Install** button

3. Tap on the **Accept** button to accept the permissions requested by the app

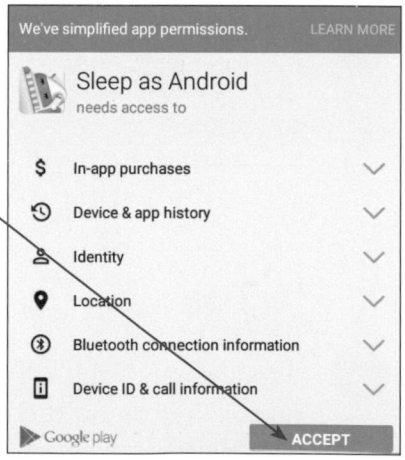

Under **Settings > Sound & notification**, tap on the **App notification** button to select apps to display their notifications in the Notifications Area.

4 The progress of the download is shown on the Apps Homepage in the Play Store (and also in the Notifications Area)

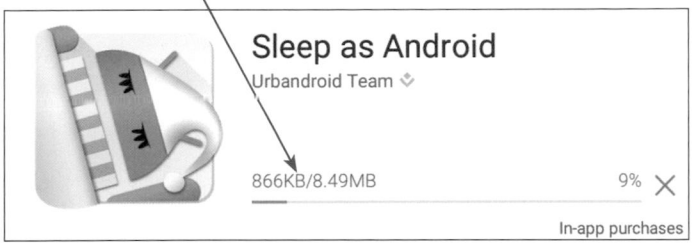

5 Newly downloaded apps are added where there is space on the next available Home screen

6 For a paid-for app, tap on the price button and tap on the **Accept** button as in Step 3 on the previous page. Tap on the **Open** button in the Play Store to open it directly from here

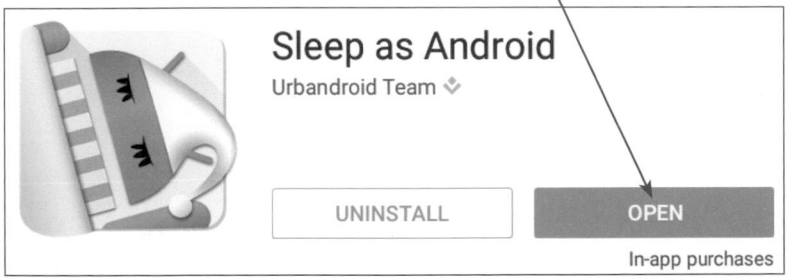

Deleting Apps

The built-in apps on an Android tablet cannot be deleted easily, but the ones that have been downloaded from the Play Store can be removed. You may want to do this if you do not use a certain app any more and you feel the number of apps on your tablet is becoming unmanageable. To delete a downloaded app:

1. Press and hold on one of the apps on the Home screen, until the Trash icon appears at the top

2. Drag the app over the Trash icon until it turns red

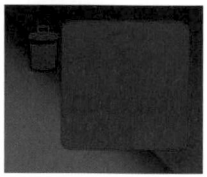

3. Tap on the **OK** button to confirm the deletion

Built-in apps have a **Disable** button instead of an **Uninstall** one in Step 3. Tap on this to stop the app's operation. This does not remove it and it can be reinstated with the corresponding **Enable** button.

Updating Apps

The world of apps is a dynamic and fast-moving one and new apps are being created and added to the Play Store on a daily basis. Existing apps are also being updated, to improve their performance and functionality. Once you have installed an app from the Play Store it is possible to obtain updates, at no extra cost (if the app was paid for). To do this:

1. Access the Play Store. Tap on the **Menu** button and then the **My apps** button

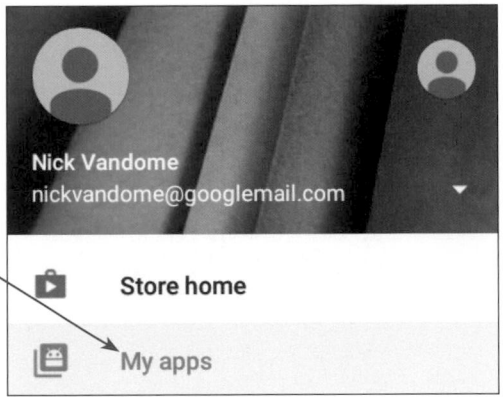

2. Tap on the **Installed** tab to view the apps on your tablet. Tap here to update all of the appropriate apps or tap on the **Update** button next to a specific app to update it

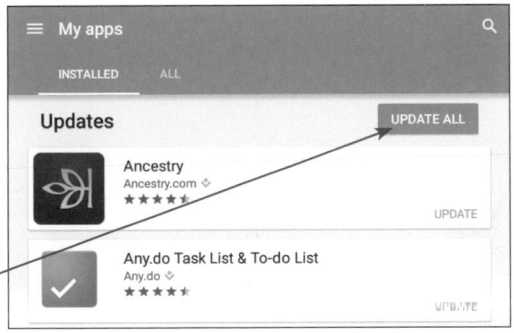

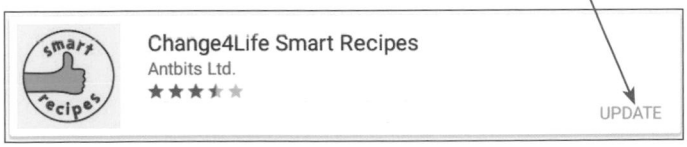

Apps are also updated to improve security features and include any fixes to improve the performance of the app.

App Information

For both built-in apps and those downloaded from the Play Store it is possible to view details about them and also see the permissions that they are using to access certain functions. To view information about your apps:

1. Open the **Settings** app and tap on the **Apps** button under **Device**

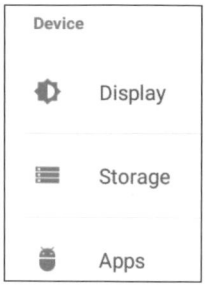

2. Tap on the **All** tab and tap on an app

3. Tap on the **Force stop** button to close a running app

4. Details about the size of the app, and the amount of data it has stored, is shown here

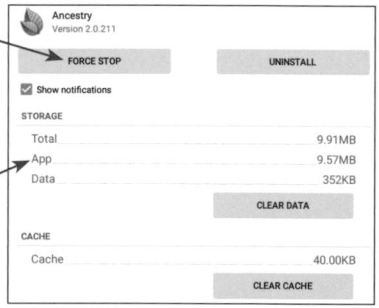

5. Swipe down to **Permissions** to view what the app is accessing on your tablet

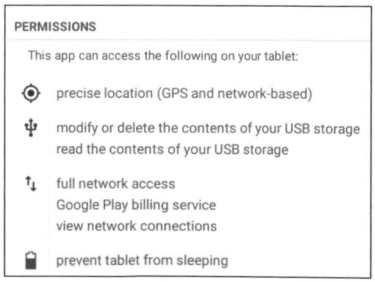

The **Clear data** button removes all of the settings for the app and the data that it has stored. The **Clear cache** button removes data that has been stored temporarily in the app's memory.

5 Useful Apps

Everyone has different interests and hobbies and this chapter looks at a range of apps for a variety of topics.

82 Staying Organized

84 Being Productive

86 Keeping Entertained

88 Lifestyle

92 Health and Fitness

96 Family History

Staying Organized

Tablets offer a lot in terms of entertainment and communication, but they are also excellent for helping to keep us organized in our everyday lives, whether it is keeping notes, making to-do lists or even finding lost items in the dark. There are also options for organizing the tablet itself.

Evernote

One of the top note-taking options, this sophisticated and powerful app delivers functionality for creating notes that can then be viewed via Evernote on a variety of other devices once you have created a new account. Photos, videos and audio clips can be added to notes.

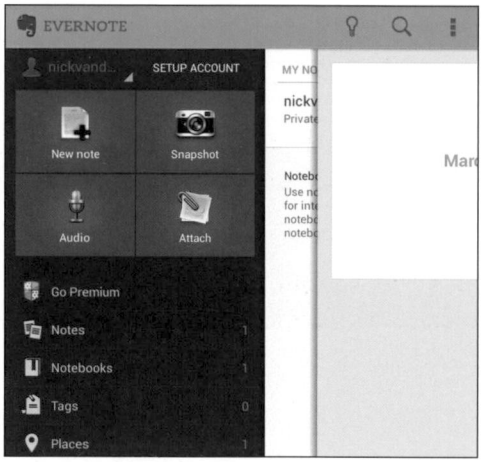

Dropbox is a great way to store and share photos, particularly when you are traveling. If you have a Wi-Fi connection you will be able to upload your photos on vacation, which is a great way to keep them safe.

Dropbox

Storing content in the 'cloud' is becoming increasingly common. This is the method of storing and sharing items on a company's computer server, rather than just on your own device. One of the best options is Dropbox and this app provides access to this method of sharing the content on your tablet. Once you have set up an account, which is free, you can upload content from your tablet which can then be accessed by yourself, or other people, from an Internet-enabled device that has Dropbox installed.

ColorNote Notepad

A simple but effective note-taking app that can be used to jot down your thoughts, ideas or lists.

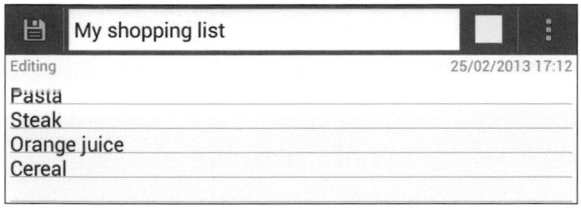

Better Notepad

Another simple, but effective, note-taking app.

Handrite Notes Notepad

A note-taking app that allows you to write the notes on the tablet's touchscreen, using either your finger or a stylus pen. It can take a bit of practice to get the handwriting looking its best but it is worth persevering with.

Any.Do

A to-do list and task reminder app that can be used to organize your daily, weekly and monthly tasks. Items can be entered using text input or speech and alerts can be set.

Flashlight LED

If you need to find or read something in the dark this app can help light your way. Use either the tablet's camera or its screen as a flashlight.

All-in-One Toolbox

An app for organizing your tablet. This can be used for a variety of housekeeping tasks, such as boosting system memory, a task killer for closing down unresponsive apps and over a dozen other tools for optimizing the performance of your tablet.

Battery Widget

A handy app for displaying details about the performance of your tablet's battery.

A lot of apps have a Lite version and a Pro version. The Lite version is free, while there is usually a charge for the Pro version. Lite versions usually have restricted functionality compared with the Pro versions.

Being Productive

Traditional productivity tasks, such as creating letters or documents with word processing, or compiling spreadsheets for things like household expenses, are well catered for on Android tablets. There are versions of the popular Microsoft productivity apps such as Word, Excel and PowerPoint, in the Play Store and also a range of other apps that can open files in these formats and create them too.

Before downloading a productivity app, check the information about it in the Play Store to make sure that it can work with Microsoft documents, if that is what you want it for. All of the Play Store productivity apps can also be used on their own to create content on your tablet.

Office suite apps usually have a file manager functionality too, where you can view and manage the files that you have created with the app.

Kingsoft Office

A free office app that still manages to support the use of 23 different file types, including all of the popular Microsoft ones: Word, Excel and PowerPoint. Documents can be created using preset templates to ensure that they are created in a suitable format.

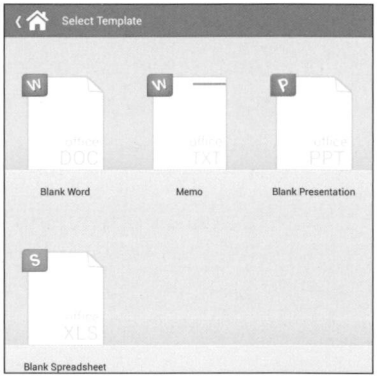

OfficeSuite Pro

A fully functioning suite of apps for word processing, speadsheets, presentations and reading PDF documents. Aimed largely at the business user, but it is still ideal for use in the home if you are going to be undertaking a range of productivity tasks.

Smart Office

Another office suite of apps that can be used to create, open and view Microsoft Office documents. It can also be used to print documents without the need for using a separate printing app (see next page).

Writer

A basic word processing app, but one that can be used to create documents that are longer than those created with a notes app. When documents are created they are automatically saved by Writer, creating a document title with the first line that has been entered.

Simple Spreadsheet

As the name suggests, a simple app for creating spreadsheets. It does not have as much functionality as some of those with the suite of apps but it can still be used for spreadsheets for items such as household expenditure or vacation expenses.

PrinterShare Mobile Print

By default there is no option for printing from most Android apps. This app can be used to print documents wirelessly by sending them, via Wi-Fi, to your printer. To achieve this you will need to have a printer that is connected to your wireless network. Open the app and select the type of item that you want to print and then select the required printer (which has to be turned on in order for the app to discover it wirelessly).

PrintHand Mobile Print

Another paid-for printing app that can be used to print Office documents, photos and emails.

Most printer manufacturers have their own apps that can be used to print on their own compatible printers.

There is a Lite version of the PrinterShare app. This only allows for printing test pages. If you want unlimited printing you will have to pay for the Premium version.

Some printer apps require you to download printer drivers to ensure that they can work with your installed printers. These are small programs that help the app and the printer talk to each other.

Keeping Entertained

There are a number of built-in Android apps that can be used for several areas of entertainment, such as reading, listening to music and watching movies. In addition, the Play Store also has hundreds of apps to add to your entertainment options.

Depending on your geographical location there will be other video subscription apps that you should be able to use with whichever subscription service you use, if applicable.

Netflix

An app for the popular website for downloading and watching movies and TV shows on your tablet. A subscription is required for the service and you can then search for and watch thousands of movies and TV shows.

IMDb Movies & TV

A comprehensive database of everything connected with movies and TV shows, including information about them, their stars and directors and clips from them. It is owned by Amazon and there are links for a lot of the items so that you can buy them directly from the Amazon website.

Social networking is now an important part of the online experience. Apps for Facebook and Twitter can be downloaded from the Play Store and used to communicate with family and friends, and provide entertainment opportunities through sharing photos and videos and playing games. See pages 140-141 for more details.

TuneIn Radio

Listen to digital radio on your tablet with this app. You can listen to stations around the world and search for content according to different categories such as music, sports, news, talk and location.

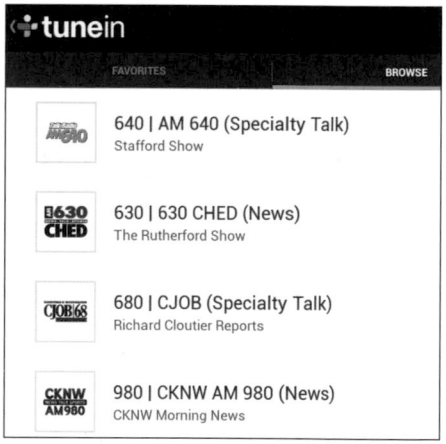

Internet Radio

An eclectic range of radio stations, broadcasting on the Internet around the world.

Magic Piano

A music app which can be used to download songs (from classical to pop) and then play along with them by following lightbeams on the virtual piano keyboard. A great way to learn the piano and play along with a variety of songs.

My Piano

Another Piano app with a virtual keyboard that can be used to learn the piano, or play your favorite tunes on your tablet if you are already a pianist.

Games

Although computer games may seem like the preserve of the younger generation this is definitely not the case. Not all computer games are of the shoot-em-up or racing variety and the Play Store also contains puzzles and versions of popular board games. Some games to try are:

- **Chess**. Pit your wits against a selection of free Chess apps. Various settings can be applied for each game, such as the level of difficulty.
- **Checkers**. Similar to the Chess apps, but for Checkers (Draughts). Hints are also available to help develop your skills and knowledge.
- **Mahjong**. A version of the popular Chinese game that can be used in single-player mode and there are also options for linking up with other online players.
- **Solitaire**. An old favorite, the card game where you have to build sequences and remove all of the cards.
- **Sudoku**. The numbers game where you have to fill different grids with numbers 1-9, without having any of the same in a row or column.
- **Tetris**. One of the original computer games, where you have to piece together falling shapes to make lines.
- **Words With Friends**. Similar to Scrabble, an online word game, played with other users.

As well as the games here, there is also a full range of other types of games in the Play Store. Two favorites are Candy Crush and Angry Birds.

Lifestyle

When it comes to hobbies and pastimes, the Play Store has apps that cover a wide range of lifestyle options.

Gardeners Calendar

For anyone who is interested in the increasingly popular pastime of growing your own vegetables. All of the information is self-contained within the app and covers all aspects of growing vegetables, with details about what you need to do at different times of the year.

Most lifestyle topics have several apps covering them. Try out different ones to see which you prefer.

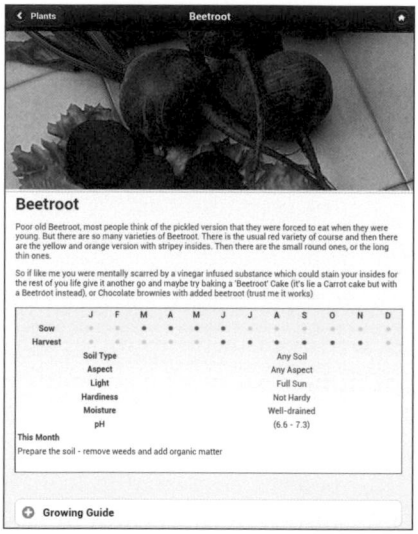

Beginners Gardening Guide

An excellent, extensive guide for anyone new to the delights of gardening. It has categories covering topics such as plant nutrients, garden design, gardening ideas, flower gardens and vegetable gardens. Even for experienced gardeners there will be some useful tips, hints and ideas here too.

BigOven 350,000+ Recipes

An app that does pretty much as it says. There are recipes for all kinds of cooking. You can also get ideas for using up leftovers by entering ingredients and then viewing the suggestions (although this is not always the most accurate).

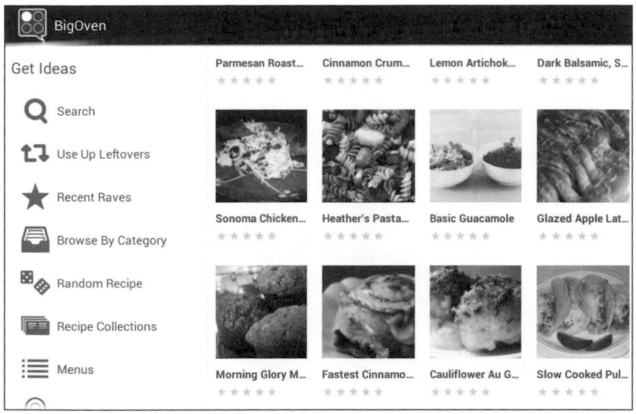

Some of the categories in BigOven come under the Pro heading, which means you have to create an account to view them, which is free to do.

Jamie's 20 Minute Meals

Mouthwatering recipes and cooking tips from TV chef Jamie Oliver. It is a paid-for app and offers numerous quick, healthy and tasty recipes and also a section for items for your shopping list for the recipes.

...cont'd

Cocktail Flow – Drink Recipes

For anyone wanting to unravel the mysteries of the cocktail maker, this is the ideal app. Dozens of cocktail recipes, listed by name, base drink, color and type. When a cocktail is selected, its ingredients are listed, along with any equipment required to make it and also preparation instructions.

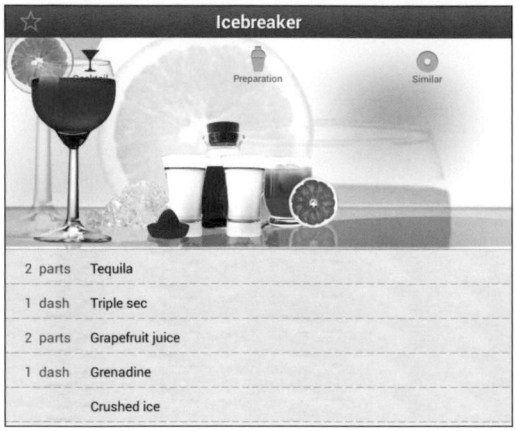

Try to keep your alcohol consumption within recommended guidelines. There are apps that you can use to keep a record of the amount you drink; see page 93.

Wine Secretary (WS) – Wine and Cellar

Wine is not only a pleasant accompaniment to food, or enjoyable on its own; it can also be an interesting hobby. This app contains details of thousands of types of wine and enables you to build up a list of all of your favorites. There is also a free wine dictionary app that can be downloaded.

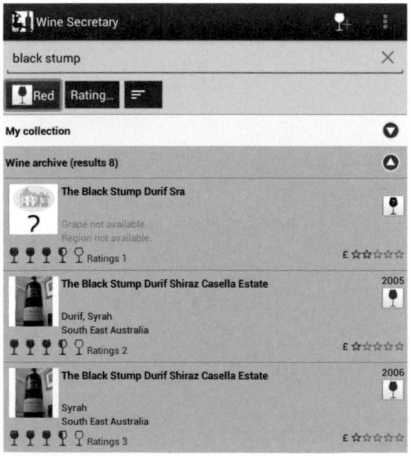

How to Draw – Easy Lessons

An excellent app for developing your drawing and painting skills. Once you have selected a drawing, you can move through it, step-by-step from the beginning, until it is completed. You can follow the steps on a sheet of paper so that when the tutorial is finished you will have your own version of the picture.

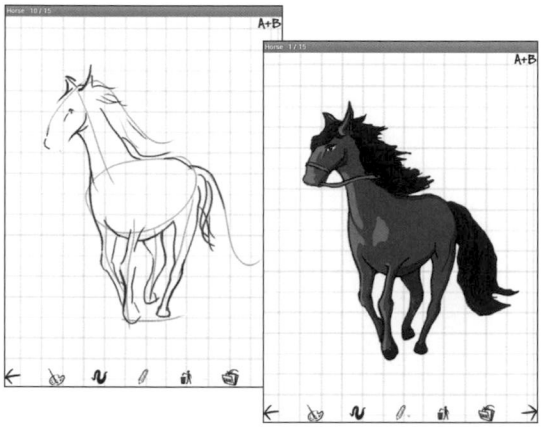

Museums

Some of the best Android apps for museums are for locating attractions in individual cities. Enter 'Museums' and the name of a city into the Play Store Search box to see if there is a museum app for that city. The majority cover US cities and their locations can also be viewed on a city map.

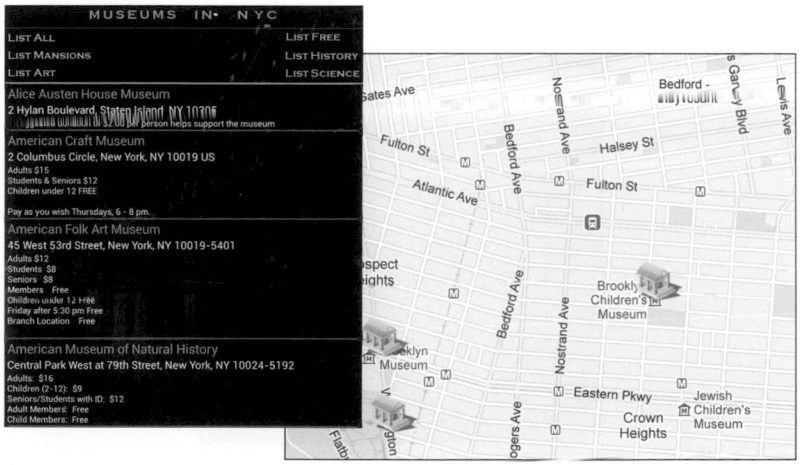

Some museums have live wallpaper apps which can be used as the background on your tablet. Enter the name of a museum, such as the Louvre, to see if there is one with live wallpaper. These tend to be images of the museum itself rather than its contents.

Health and Fitness

Keeping fit and healthy should be a fun and varied part of life. In the Play Store there are apps covering areas to ensure that you have a good time keeping in shape.

Simply Yoga

Yoga is excellent exercise which is beneficial for overall fitness and flexibility. This app has video demonstrations of different techniques and there is also a spoken commentary that leads you through each one.

For the yoga and workout apps, the videos can be paused by tapping on the button in the middle, at the top of the screen. Tap it again to continue.

Daily Workouts

Similar to the yoga app, this one contains a range of exercises with the same video walk-through format. Exercises can be selected for different parts of the body.

Change4Life Smart Recipes

Healthy eating need not be dull and this app provides a wealth of tasty, healthy recipes, as well as general information about nutrition and eating well.

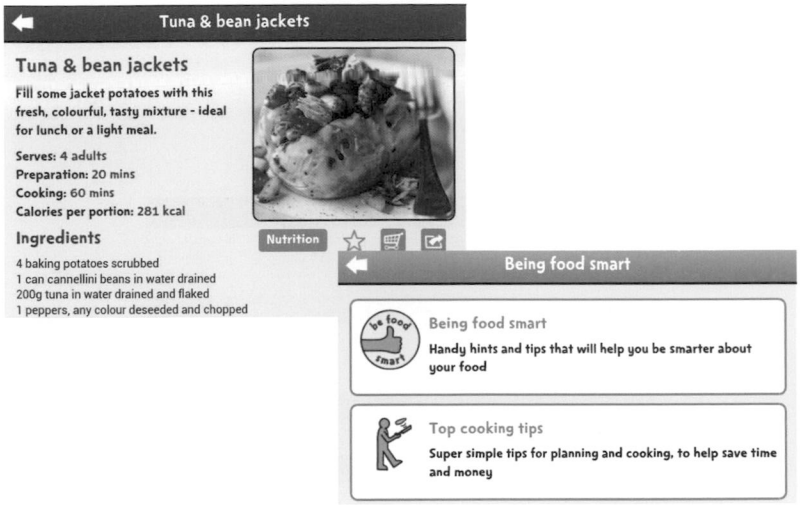

Change4Life Drinks Tracker

Although drinking can be a very enjoyable pastime, it is a good idea to note down how much you are drinking, so that you can keep it within safe limits. This app allows you to compile a record of your daily consumption and has guidelines about safe drinking levels.

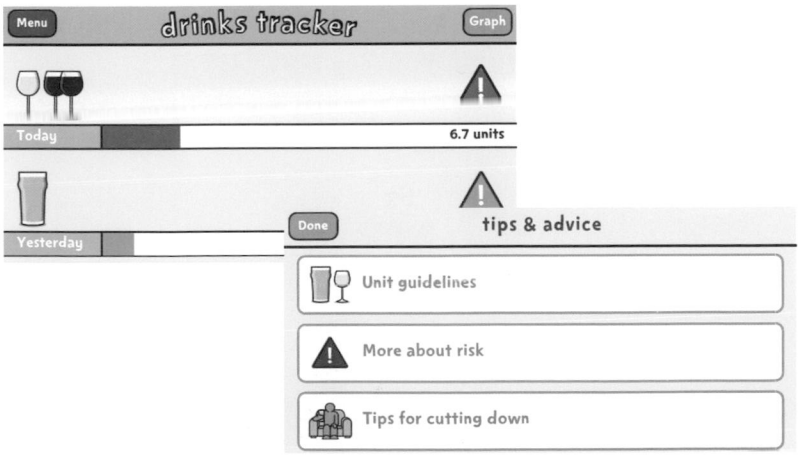

If you are using any drinks tracker app, make sure that you fill it in accurately and honestly to ensure that you get a genuine overall picture.

...cont'd

Calorie Counter – My FitnessPal

There are several calorie counter apps in the Play Store, to help give you an idea of the balance between your calorie intake and the amount of energy that you are using with exercise. They all work in a similar way in that you have to register with the app, set a target weight and then enter your daily calorie intake and amount of exercise. The app will then keep you up-to-date with whether you are on course to achieve your target weight loss.

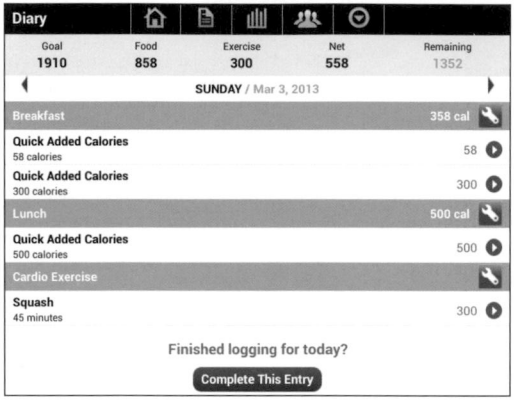

RunKeeper – GPS Track Run Walk

Combined with the GPS on your tablet, this app can be used to log the distance that you have completed during exercise. It can also be used to set up a training plan if you want to undertake a specific type of event, such as a fun run.

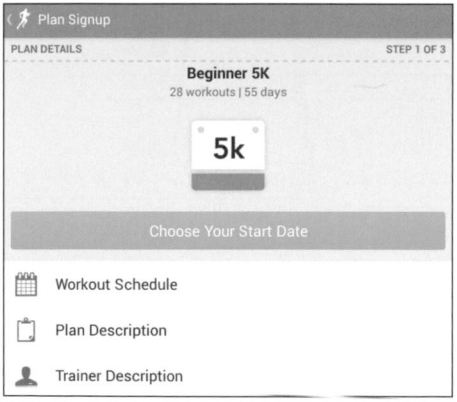

Make sure the Location services is turned on if you want to use the RunKeeper app. This can be found in **Settings > Personal > Location** and drag the **Location** button to On.

First aid by the British Red Cross

An excellent reference for general first aid. Compiled by the world-renowned British Red Cross, it contains videos, diagrams and advice about a range of medical situations. There is also an Emergency button that can be used for specific advice if you are in a life-threatening situation.

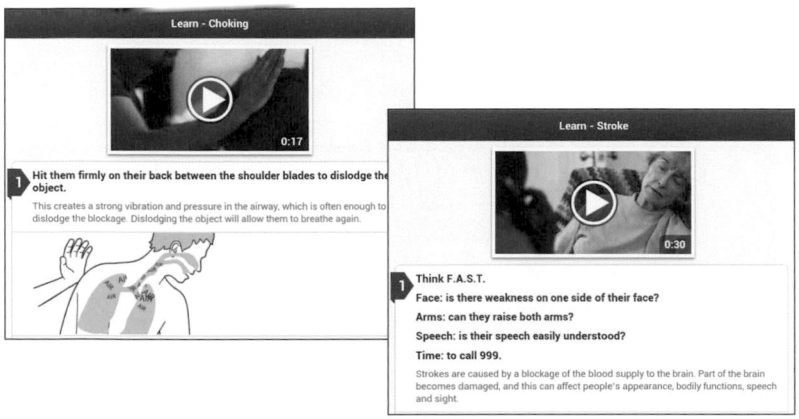

Getting medical advice on the Internet or through apps is no substitute for consulting with your own doctor. If you are worried about something, speak to your doctor first.

Nature Sounds Relax and Sleep

Getting a good night's sleep is one of the foundations of good general health. This app provides a range of soothing sounds from nature, such as waterfalls, birdsong and forest sounds, to help you get to sleep. There is also a timer that can be set so that the app turns off after a certain period of time so that it is not playing all night.

Family History

Researching family history has enjoyed a remarkable growth since it became possible to check up details on the Internet. This has now extended to tablet apps, which you can use to create family trees.

Ancestry

This app is linked to the Ancestry website. The app can be used to create your own family tree, but you have to create an account on the relevant Ancestry website for your location in order to be able to search historical records.

Researching family history can be a compelling hobby and once you start you may find that you want to keep looking further and further into your family background.

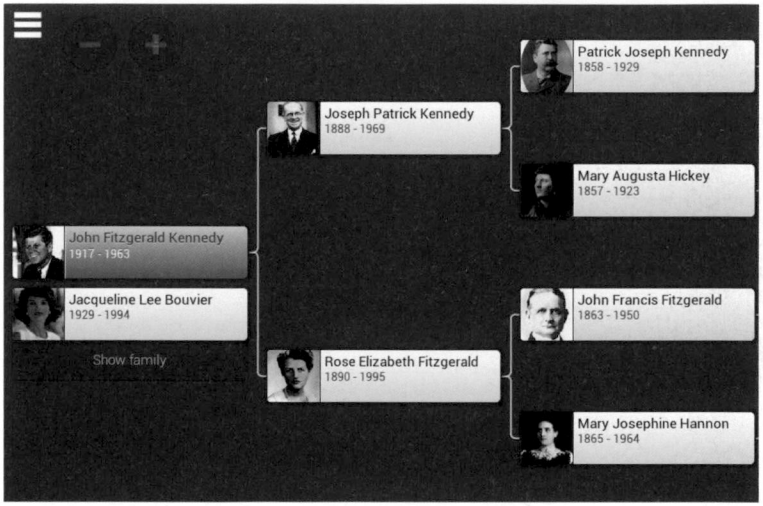

FamilySearch Tree

Similar to the Ancestry app in that it links to the **FamilySearch.org** website for registered users of this service. People, photos, text and also video can be added to the family trees that are created here.

Family Tree

Not strictly a family history app, this enables you to create a family sharing environment within Facebook, where family members can share information and also access a shared calendar for family events.

6 Tablet Entertainment

Android tablets are not only useful; they are also great fun. This chapter shows how to make the most of your tablet as your own personal entertainment center. It details how to obtain, manage & listen to music, download and watch movies & TV shows, read all of your favorite books and magazines, take photos then view, manage, edit and share your digital images.

98 Using Google Play
99 Music on Android
100 Downloading Music
102 Transferring Music
104 Playing Music
107 Managing Music
108 Pinning Music
110 Movies and TV Shows
114 Obtaining Books
116 Around an Ebook
118 Adding Notes
120 Adding Bookmarks
121 Definitions and Translations
122 Using Cameras
124 Adding Photos
127 Viewing Photos
130 Editing Photos
132 Sharing Photos

Using Google Play

Google Play is the online store for buying, downloading, using and managing a range of entertainment content. It is accessed at the website:

- **play.google.com**

You need to have a Google Account in order to log in to the Google Play website.

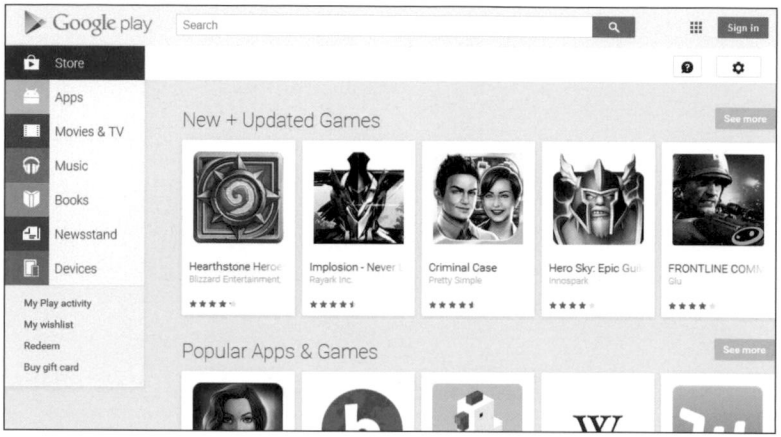

Content that is downloaded to your Android tablet via the Play Store will also be available on the Google Play website, as long as you are logged in with your Google Account.

Once you have logged in to Google Play you can download a variety of content:

- Music
- Books
- Magazines
- Movies
- Apps

Content from Google Play is stored in the cloud so it can then be used on your computer and also your Android tablet. If you delete it from your tablet, either accidentally or on purpose, you can still reinstall it from Google Play. You can also use content downloaded by any of your other Android devices, such as a smartphone.

Music on Android

One option for playing music on an Android tablet is the Play Music app. It can be used to play music that has been obtained in a number of different ways:

- Downloaded directly to your tablet from the **Play Store**.

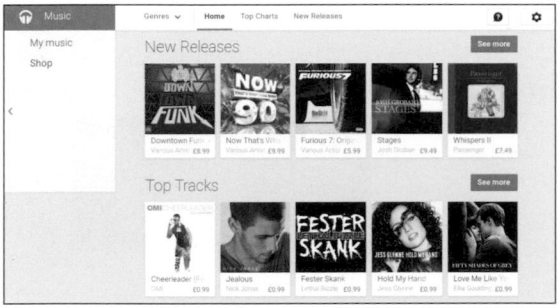

- Bought on **Google Play** and then used on your tablet.
- Uploaded to **Google Play** and then downloaded to your tablet. This can be done with the **Music Manager** that can be installed from Google Play.

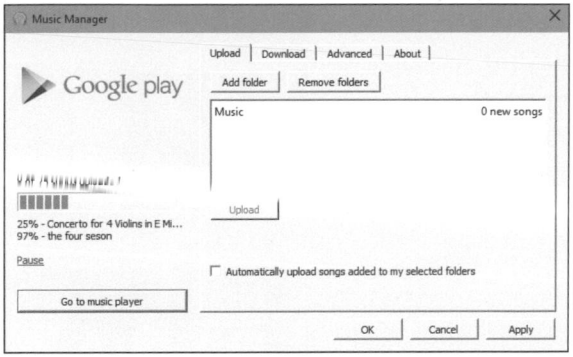

- Transferred from your computer directly to your tablet. This is done by connecting your tablet to your computer, using the USB cable, and copying your music to the **Music** folder on your tablet.
- Transferred from another mobile device using Bluetooth.

If you buy music from either the Play Store or the Google Play website, it can be played on your tablet with streaming (using a Wi-Fi Internet connection) or it can be downloaded (pinned) onto your tablet so that you can also listen to it offline (see pages 108-109).

Whenever you buy music on Google Play, or upload it from your computer, it will appear in the My Music section.

Downloading Music

To use your tablet directly to find and download music from the Play Store:

In some cases, there may be sample content in the Play Music app to help you get started with playing music.

1. Tap on the **Play Music** app to open the music player

2. Tap on the **Menu** button to access the Play Music menu, including the **Shop** button

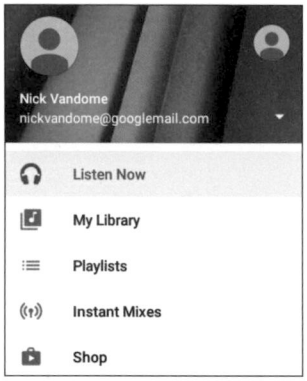

3. Use these button to view the relevant sections within the Music section of the Play Store, or

4. Tap on these sections to view the recommended content, or

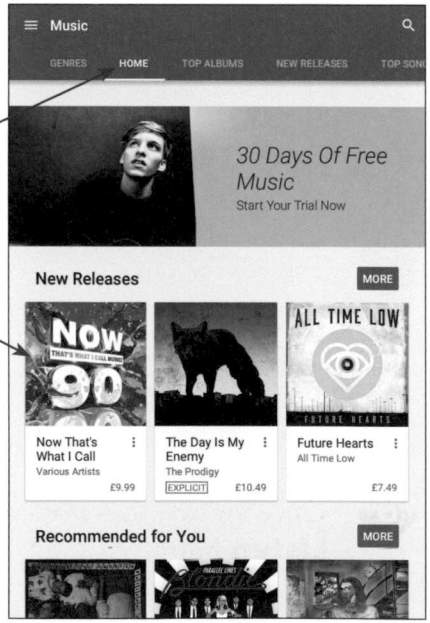

5. Tap on this button and enter an artist, album or song name into the Search box

6. Locate the item you want to download. For an album, tap on this button to buy the full album or tap on the price button next to an individual song

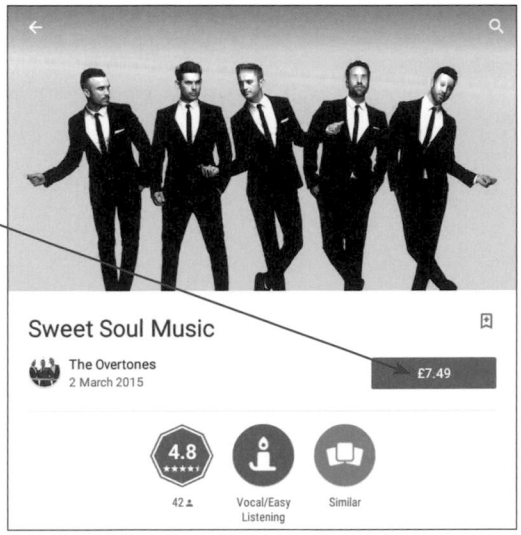

When you buy music from the Play Store it also comes with the related artwork such as album or single covers.

Songs		PLAY ALL
▶ Sweet Soul Music	02:34	£0.99
2 Get Ready	02:57	£0.99
3 Give Me Just A Little More Time	03:14	£0.99
4 Something Good	03:12	£0.99

7. Tap on the **Buy** button and enter your Google account password

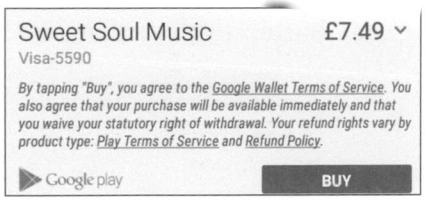

8. Once an item has been downloaded, tap on the **Listen** button to listen to it on your tablet

Transferring Music

Music does not have to be bought from the Play Store or the Google Play website in order to listen to it on your tablet. You can use music that you already have and transfer it onto your tablet. This can be done via the Google Play website.

Transferring via Google Play

Your own music can be uploaded to the Google Play website and it will then become available on your tablet. Log in to Google Play with your Google Account details.

The Music Manager app is quite small in terms of size and should not take too long to download to your computer.

1. Click on the **Music > My Music** button and then the **My Library** button

2. Click on the **Upload music** button

3. The Music Manager app is used for adding your music to Google Play. Click on this button to download it

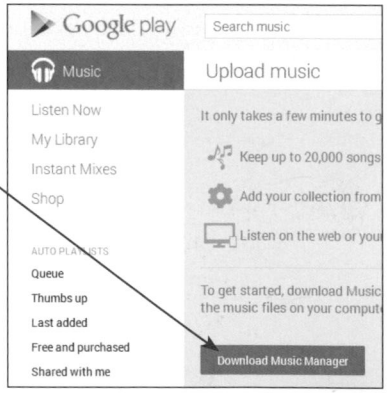

4. On your computer, click on this button to open the **Music Manager**

5 The Music Manager automatically scans your music folders and uploads them. Click on a folder to add all of the music from that location and click on the **Next** button to follow the steps for uploading

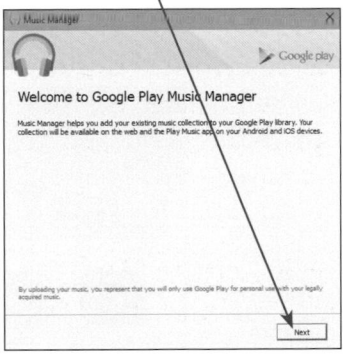

6 The progress of the upload is shown in the left-hand panel. Check on this checkbox to have new music uploaded automatically when it is added to the selected music folders on your computer

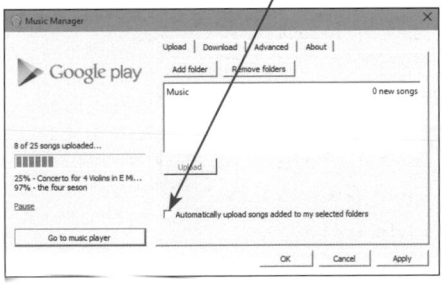

7 Once music is uploaded it is available under the **My Music** section of your Google Play account. It is also made available on your tablet through the Play Music app and your Google account

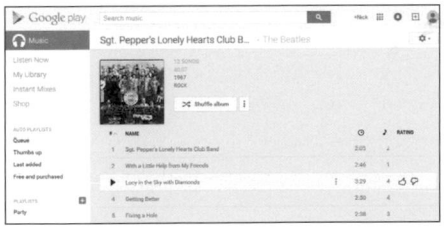

The Music Manager does not support DRM (Digital Rights Management) AAC files, which are often used in iTunes. These files will have to be converted into another format, for example MP3, before they are uploaded by the Music Manager.

Playing Music

Once you have obtained music on your tablet, by whatever means, you can then start playing it and listening to it. To do this:

1. Tap on the **Play Music** app

2. All of the available music is displayed. This includes music from the Google Play website that is only available for streaming at this point, i.e. it needs a Wi-Fi connection to play it

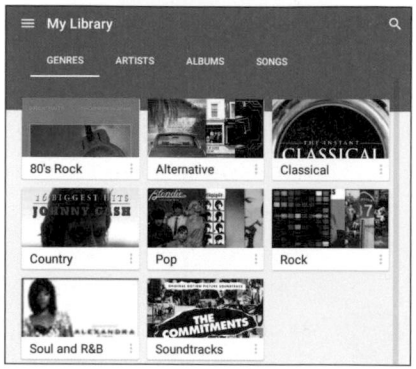

3. Tap on these buttons to view your music content according to **Genres**, **Artists**, **Albums** and **Songs**

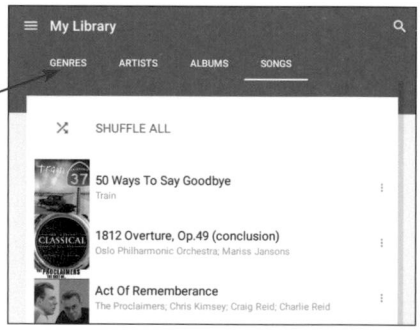

4. Tap on an item to view the available songs (for an album) or individual tracks

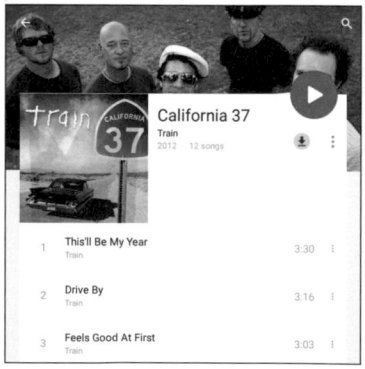

Streaming is a process where digital content is sent to a device over Wi-Fi when it is needed, in order for it to be played continuously on the device. It does not physically download the content onto the device and it remains on the server from where it was streamed.

5 Tap on a song to play it. The currently-playing song is also displayed at the bottom of the Play Music app

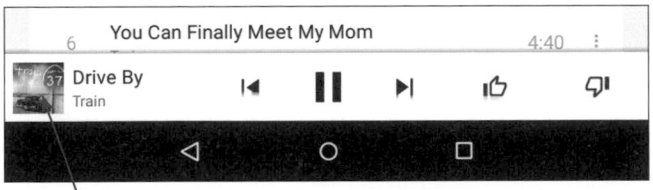

6 Tap on the song or album icon to view the song artwork at full size and view the standard playback controls at the bottom of the window

Invest in a reasonable set of headphones to listen to music on your Android tablet. This will usually result in a higher quality sound than through the built-in speakers.

7 When a song is playing, this button appears next to it

...cont'd

Music controls

When a song is playing there are several options:

1. Use these buttons to, from left to right, go back to the beginning of a song, Pause/Play a song, go to the end of a song, i.e. start playing the next one in your music library

2. For an album, tap on this button to view the current queue of songs

3. Tap in the middle of the screen to access other controls

4. Drag this button to move through a song

5. Tap on this button to shuffle the songs in your collection

6. Tap on this button to loop the currently-queued songs

7. Tap on these buttons to rate the song on the Google Play website

Queued songs are those waiting to be played in the Play Music app.

Managing Music

When you are playing music there is still a certain amount of flexibility in terms of managing what is playing, and being scheduled to play. This is known as the music queue. To use this to manage your music:

1. Tap on this button next to an album or a song

2. Tap on the **Add to queue** button to add it to the current queue of songs

3. View the song queue as shown at Step 2 on the previous page and tap on this button to hide it

4. When viewing the current queue, tap on the **Menu** button

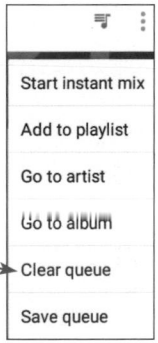

5. Tap on the **Clear queue** button to remove all of the songs from the current queue

6. When viewing the songs in the queue, tap on the same button as in Step 1 and make one of the related selections, including **Remove from queue**

When viewing the current queue, press and hold on the bar to the left of the song title and drag it to reorder its position in the current queue.

If you select **Clear queue**, this closes the currently-playing item. However, it does not remove it from your tablet and it remains available in the Play Music app.

Pinning Music

Music that is bought from the Play Store or the Google Play website is available for streaming on your tablet using your Wi-Fi Internet connection. This means that the music is sent from the Google servers, where it is stored. This means that it is always backed up and always available.

However, if you are not able to use Wi-Fi you will probably still want to listen to your music, such as when you are traveling. This can be done by pinning the required music to your tablet so that it is physically stored there. To do this:

Items that are not pinned to your device will not be available when you do not have a Wi-Fi connection.

1. Access the Play Music Menu and toggle On or Off the **Downloaded only** button to view the music on your tablet that has already been downloaded to it, rather than just being stored within the Google cloud (i.e. the server that keeps the music that you have bought)

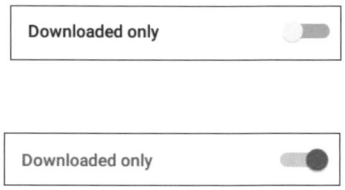

2. For **Downloaded only** the items that are stored on your tablet are shown, with an orange icon. Those that are just stored in the Google cloud will not have the orange icon displayed next to them

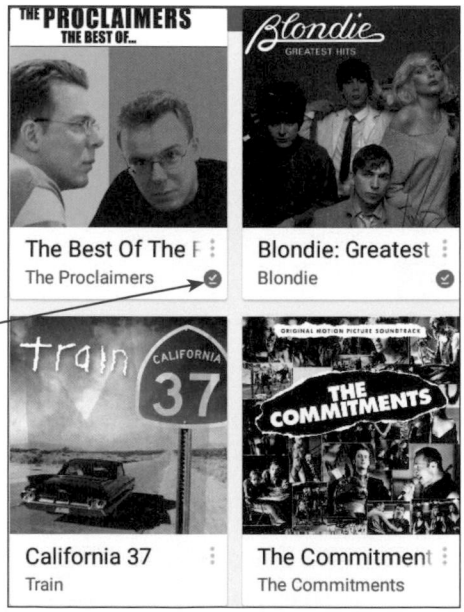

3. The icons denote the status of each item according to whether it is downloaded to the device or not. A grayed-out button indicates an item that has been accessed from the Play Store or Google Play website but has not been downloaded to the device. An orange button with a white tick indicates that an item has been downloaded to your tablet, i.e. pinned

4. Tap on a grayed-out button so that the pin turns orange, to start the process for pinning the item to your tablet

5. The item will be downloaded for storing on your tablet. This is indicated in the Notifications bar by the pin icon

6. Swipe down on the Notifications bar to see the progress of the track(s) being downloaded

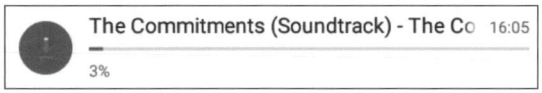

7. Tap on an item in Step 6 to view the full download queue

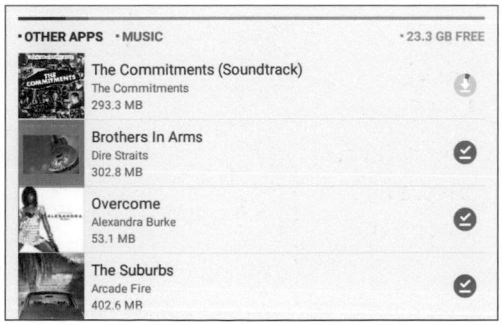

The more music that you download to your tablet, the more storage space it will take up.

Movies and TV Shows

There are different ways in which video content can be viewed on your Android tablet:

- Downloading movies and TV shows from the Play Store or the Google Play website
- Transferring (uploading) your own videos to your tablet
- Watching videos on YouTube

To obtain movies or TV shows from the Play Store:

Some tablets have their own default movies app, which will be linked to their own app store. If this is the case, the Play Movies app can still be downloaded from the Play Store, and content can be bought from there.

1. Tap on the **Play Movies & TV** app

2. Tap here and tap on the **My Library** button to view available content on your tablet. This includes movies and TV shows that you have downloaded, and also recommended titles

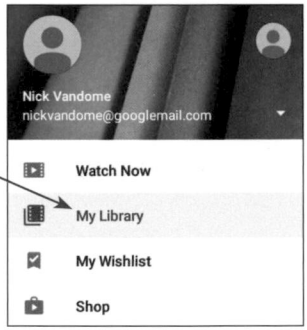

When buying or renting items from the Play Store there are usually options for doing so in Standard Definition (SD) or High Definition (HD).

3. Tap on an item in the **My Movies** section to view it

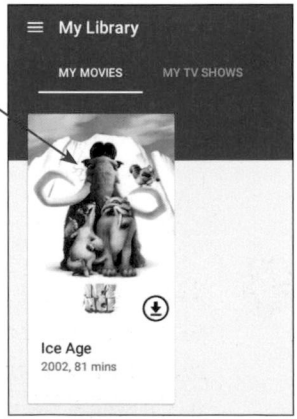

4. Tap on the **Shop** button in Step 2 to view the available movies and TV shows in the Play Store

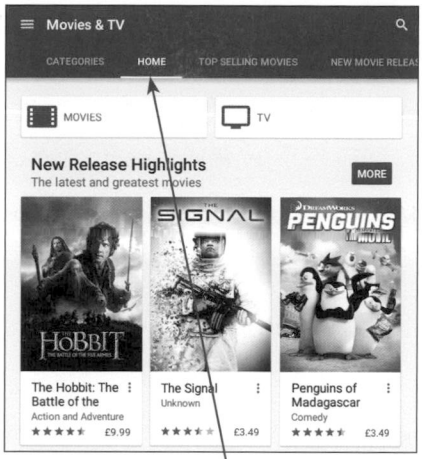

5. The **Movies** section of the Play Store is similar to those for the other types of content. Tap on these buttons to view movies and TV shows according to these headings

Swipe to the right on the top bar to view the **Categories** section. These include Action & Adventure, Animation, Comedy, Drama, Documentary, Family and Horror.

6. Tap on the main panels to view highlighted or recommended movies and TV shows

7. Tap on an item to view details about it. Tap here to watch a preview clip

The menu options in the Movies section of the Play Store include adding the currently-viewed title to a Wishlist for buying or downloading later, redeeming a voucher, viewing your account details, viewing general Play Store settings and help options.

8. Tap on these buttons to buy or rent a movie or TV show. This will be made available within the Play Movies app

RENT FROM £3.49 | BUY FROM £9.99

...cont'd

9 Tap on the **Rent** (or **Buy**) button to accept the Play Store terms and conditions

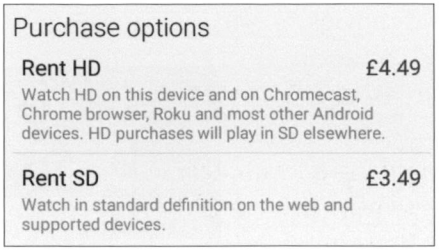

10 Enter your Google Account password and tap on the **Confirm** button to complete the purchase

11 Tap on the **Play** button to start playing your purchase. This is done by streaming it from the Internet using Wi-Fi. Tap on the **Download** button to download the item to your tablet so that you can play it at any time, even if you are not connected to the Internet

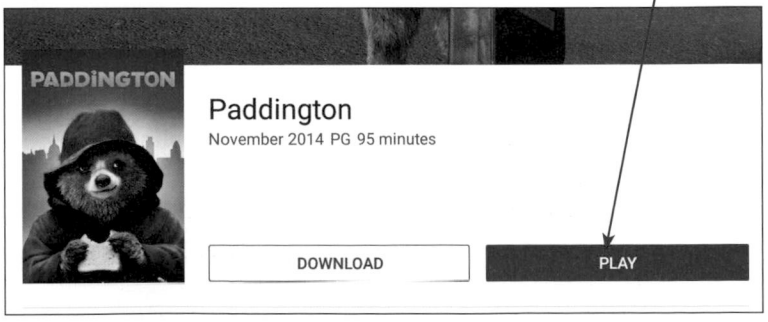

If you rent a movie or a TV show it has to be started within 30 days of being rented and watched within 48 hours of when it was first started.

Video clips can also be viewed online with the built-in YouTube app.

Watching movies and TV shows

When you have bought, or rented, movies or TV shows you can then watch them on your tablet:

1. Open the **Play Movies & TV** app and view your rented and bought content under the **My Library** section. Tap on the item you want to view

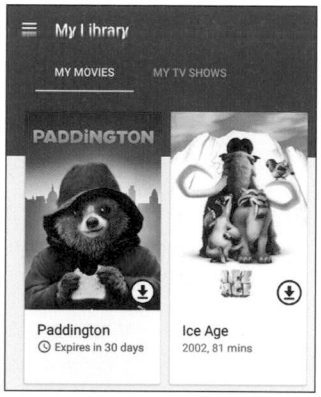

2. Tap on the **Play** button to start watching a movie or TV show

3. For rented items you have 48 hours to watch them after you start watching. Tap on the **OK** button to start

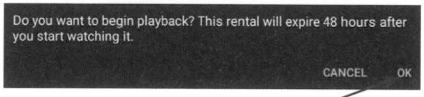

4. By default, movies and TV shows are streamed from the Play Store. Tap on the **Download** button to store the content on your tablet so that you can watch it offline

Use an HDMI cable with your tablet so that you can watch movies and TV shows on a High Definition TV.

If you download movies and TV shows to your tablet they can take up a considerable amount of storage space. Rented items will be automatically deleted once the rental period expires.

Obtaining Books

Due to their size and portability, Android tablets are ideal for reading ebooks. There is a wide range that can be downloaded from the Play Store, or from the Google Play website, in a similar way to obtaining music, movies and apps.

The Books section can also be accessed from the main Homepage of the **Play Store** by tapping on the **Books** button at the top of the screen.

1. Tap on the **Play Books** app (or access the Google Play website)

2. Any books that you already have on your tablet are displayed. Tap on a cover to open a specific title

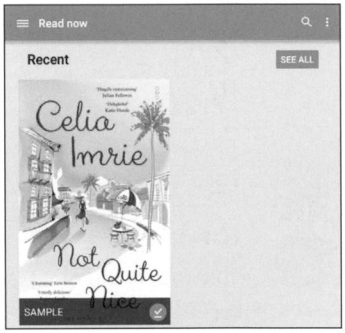

Swipe left and right at the top of the window to access the different main headings.

3. Tap on the **Menu** button and tap on the **Shop** button

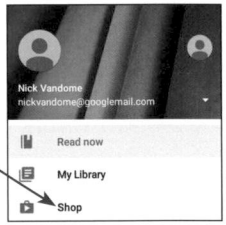

The Kindle app can be downloaded from the Play Store for reading books. If you already have a Kindle account your books will be available through the Kindle app on your tablet.

4. Books can be browsed for and downloaded in a similar way as for other Play Store content. Tap on these buttons to view books according to these headings

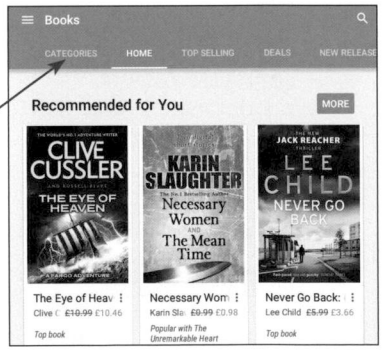

5. Tap on the main panels to view highlighted or recommended books

6 When you find a book you want to read, tap on the **Free Sample** button (if there is one) or the **Buy** button (with the price)

7 When any book from the Play Books store has been downloaded to your tablet it is available within your Play Books library

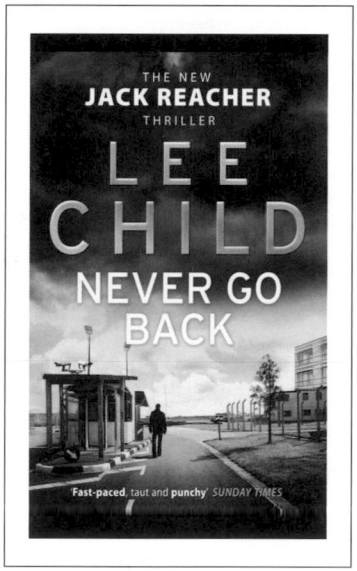

8 Tap in the middle of the page to access the reading controls

One of the categories in the Play Store Books section is for Top Free books. Some classic titles also have free versions if the copyright has expired after a certain period of time following the author's death.

Check out the ebook version of this title and other **In Easy Steps** ebooks in the Play Store. Samples for all titles are downloadable for free:

Around an Ebook

Once you have downloaded ebooks to your tablet you can start reading them. Due to their format there is a certain amount of electronic functionality that is not available in a hard copy version. To find your way around your ebook:

You can also move to the next or previous page by tapping at the right-hand or left-hand edge of a page.

1. Swipe left and right on a page to move backwards or forwards by one page

2. Tap in the middle of a page to access the reading controls toolbars at the top and bottom of the screen

3. Drag this button to move through the book

4. Tap on this button to access the book's table of contents. Tap on a heading to move to that point in the book

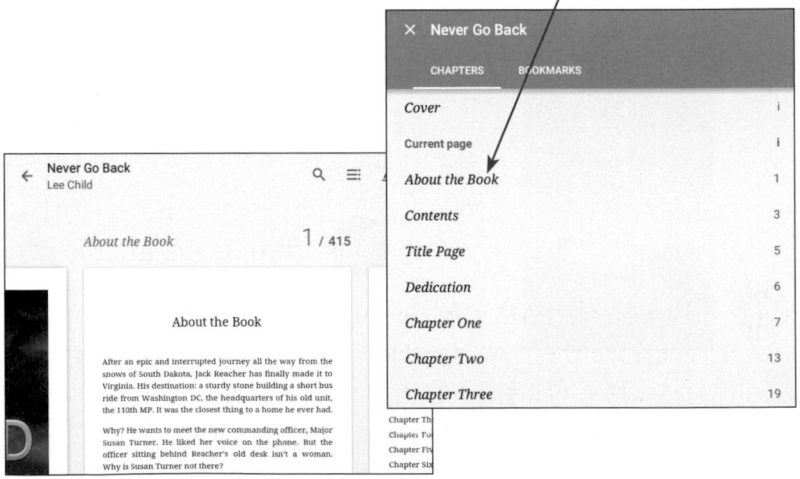

To delete an ebook from the Play Books app, press and hold on its cover and tap on the **Remove from my library** button. The book can be reinstalled from the Play Store if you want to place it in your library again. This is free to do.

5 Tap on the **Menu** button to access the specific settings for the title you are reading

6 Some older books have an option for reading it in its original format. Tap on the **Original pages** button to view this

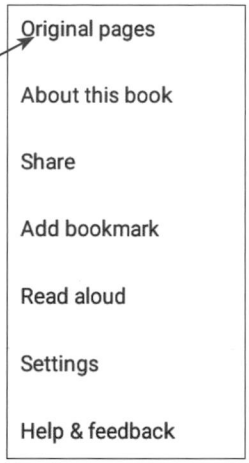

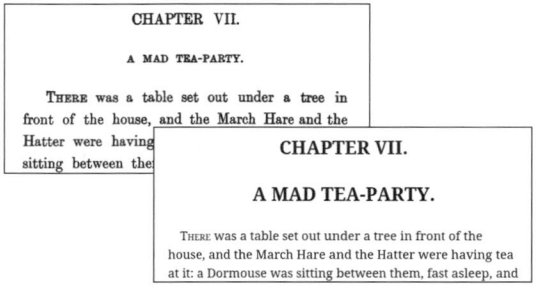

To go back to the standard Play Books format from the Original pages, tap on the button in Step 5 and tap on the **Flowing text** button.

7 Tap on this button to select text options

8 Tap on these buttons to select black text on a white background, white text on a black background, or Sepia

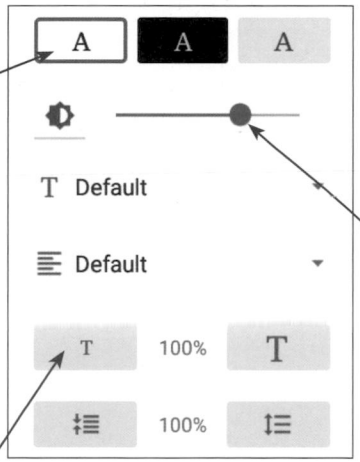

Drag on the **Brightness** button in Step 8 to change the screen brightness for your book.

9 Tap on the **Font Size** buttons to increase or decrease the font size by one step each time. Tap on the **Line Height** buttons (below the text buttons) to increase or decrease the space between lines

Adding Notes

If you like taking notes while you are reading books you no longer have to worry about jotting down your thoughts in the margins or on pieces of paper. With Play Books ebooks you can add your own electronic notes and also insert bookmarks at your favorite passages. To do this:

1. Press and hold on a word to activate the two blue text selection markers

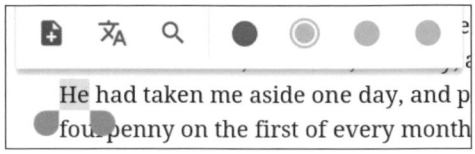

2. Drag one of the blue markers over the text to select it and access the top toolbar

When text is selected, tap on one of the colors on the toolbar to change the color with which it is highlighted.

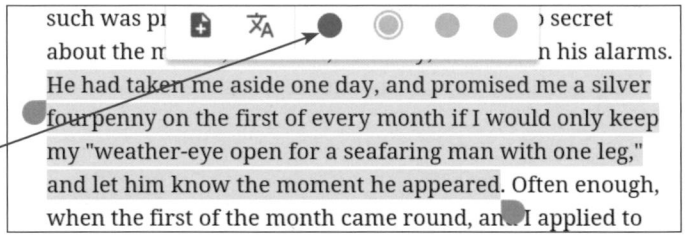

3. Tap on this button to add a note

4. Enter a note for the selected text and tap on the **Save** button on the top toolbar

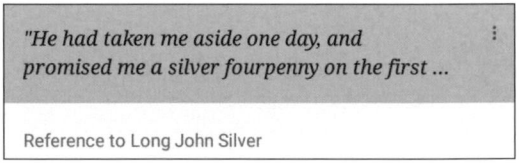

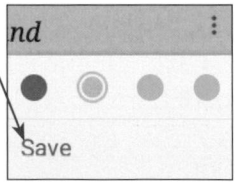

5. A note is indicated by a small yellow icon next to the highlighted text. Tap on this to edit the note

He had taken me aside one day, and promised me a silver fourpenny on the first of every month if I would only keep my "weather-eye open for a seafaring man with one leg," and let him know the moment he appeared. Often enough,

6. To view all of your notes, tap on the **Table of Contents** button and tap on the **Notes** tab

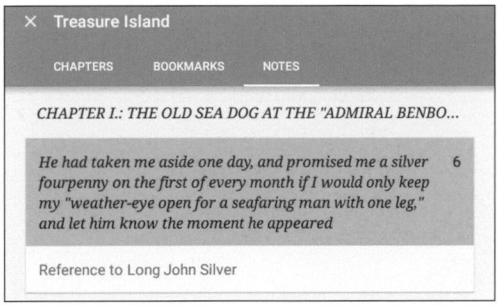

7. Notes are shown on the **Notes** page. Tap on an item to go to that point in the book

8. To delete a note, access it in the book and tap on the yellow note icon and tap on the **Menu** button

9. On the top toolbar, tap on the **Delete** button

10. Tap on the **Remove** button to confirm the action

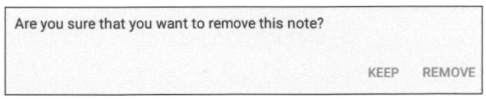

Adding Bookmarks

One of the great things about a hard copy book is that you can physically mark pages, or insert a bookmark, so that you can keep your place. However, with ebooks this functionality has been added so that you can bookmark as many pages as you like, for quick access.

You can add numerous bookmarks throughout a book. However, if you add too many the **Bookmarks** tab may become cluttered and it will be harder to find items.

1. To bookmark a page in a book, tap in the top right-hand corner. A blue bookmark icon appears. Tap again to remove it

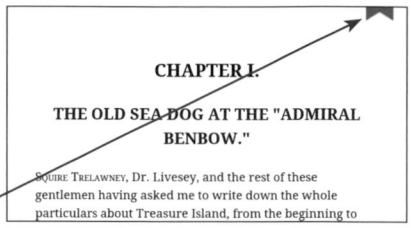

2. Bookmarks can also be added at any time by tapping on the **Menu** button and tapping on the **Add bookmark** button (once a bookmark has been added this action can be used to remove a bookmark too)

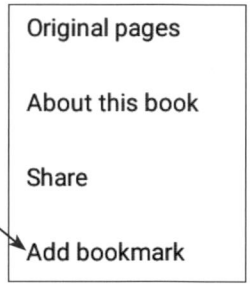

3. Bookmarks are included under the **Table of Contents** button. Tap on the **Bookmarks** tab to view the available bookmarks

4. Tap on a bookmark to go to that location

Definitions and Translations

Finding definitions

It is always satisfying to learn the meaning of new words and when reading an ebook on your tablet this can be done at any point in the text:

1. Press and hold on the word for which you want the definition

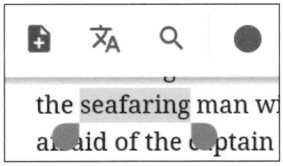

2. The definition appears at the bottom of the screen. Drag the box upwards to view it at the top of the page

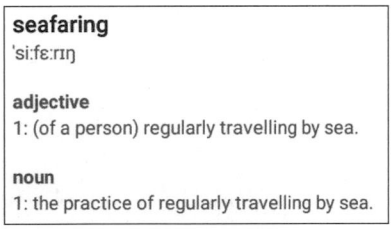

Translations

To see what the text of a book looks like in a different language, use the **Translate** option:

1. Press and hold on a word and drag one of the markers to highlight a piece of text

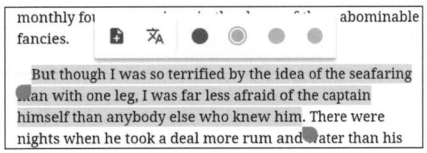

2. Tap on the **Translate** button

3. Tap on this button to select a language

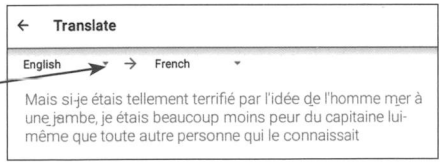

4. The translation is shown beneath the two selected languages

The translation option can be slightly hit-or-miss at times, so don't rely on it for any important translation tasks or projects.

Using Cameras

Most tablets have their own built-in camera, which can be used to capture photos directly onto the device. The quality of these vary between makes of tablet: some are good quality cameras intended to be used for taking photos in a range of conditions. Others are mainly for use as a webcam for video calls (these are front-facing cameras). To use the camera:

1. Tap on the **Camera** app 

2. The Camera app displays the current scene and the control buttons are displayed at the side (landscape view) or at the bottom (portrait view)

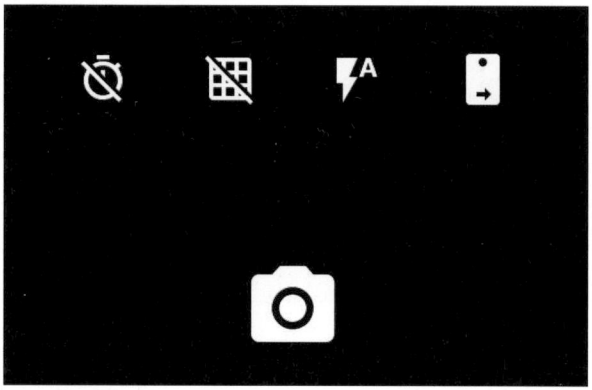

By default, photos captured with the Camera are displayed in the **Photos** app.

3. If the camera controls are not visible, tap on this button to show them 

4. Press once on the screen to focus the current scene 

5. Tap on this button to take a photo 

6. Tap on this button to switch between the front- and rear-facing cameras

7. Tap on this button to access the self-timer option

8. Tap on this button to access the settings for how the flash operates

9. Tap on this button to toggle on and off a grid over the screen, for composing photos

10. Swipe inwards from the left of the screen to access the camera options, including those for creating special effects (**Photo Sphere** and **Lens Blur**) and **Panorama**. Tap on the **Camera** or **Video** buttons to access these functions

11. When the camera options are displayed, tap on this button to access the camera's settings, including those for the resolution and quality of the images that are captured

Swipe from right to left on the main camera screen to view photos that have just been taken.

Adding Photos

Android tablets are great for storing and, more importantly, displaying your photos. The screen size of most tablets is ideal for looking at photos and you can quickly transform it into your own mobile photo album. In addition, it is also possible to share all of your photos in a variety of ways.

If you keep a lot of photos on your tablet this will start to take up its storage space.

Obtaining photos

You can get photos onto your tablet in a number of ways:

- Transferring photos from your computer directly to your tablet, via a USB cable.
- Transferring photos from your camera to your tablet. This is usually done by inserting your camera's memory card into a card reader connected to your computer and then transferring your photos.
- Copying photos from an email.
- Transferring photos from another device via Bluetooth.

Once you have captured or transferred photos to your tablet you can then view, edit and share them using the **Photos** app. Photos in the Photos app are stored in different albums, which are created automatically when photos are taken, transferred or downloaded from an email.

Personal videos can also be transferred in the same way as with photos. Copy them into the **Movies** folder of your tablet, as in Step 5 on next page, and use the **Photos** app to view them.

Transferring photos

To transfer photos to your tablet directly from a computer or your camera's memory card:

1. Connect your tablet to the computer with the supplied USB cable

2. Access your photos on your computer, or insert the camera's memory card into a card reader and access this as an external device on your computer

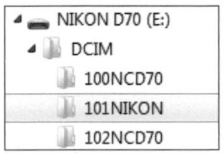

3. Copy the photos that you want to transfer

4. Access your tablet in your computer's file structure

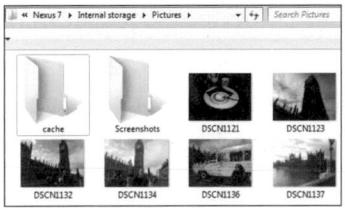

5. Navigate to the **Pictures** folder within **Internal Storage** and paste the copied photos here

6. Open the **Photos** app on your tablet to view the photos

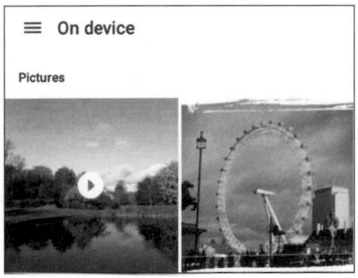

Photos copied directly from a camera's memory card will usually be in the JPEG file format, as will be the ones taken by the tablet's own camera.

Photos can also be copied straight from the camera if it is connected to the computer with a USB cable.

...cont'd

Copying from email

Email is a good method of obtaining photos on your tablet; other people can send their photos to you in this way and you can also email your own photos from a computer, a smartphone or another mobile device. To use photos from email:

1. Open the email containing the photo and tap on this button to download it

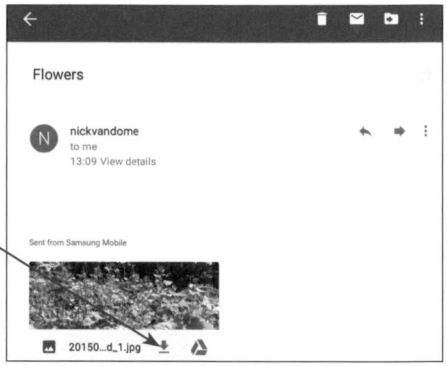

2. The photo will be saved in the **Download** folder within the **Photos** app. This will be created if it is not already there

3. Tap on the photo to open it at full size in the Photos app

Once the **Download** folder has been created all other photos downloaded from emails will be placed here.

Viewing Photos

Once you have obtained photos on your Android tablet you can start viewing, managing and editing them.

1. Open the **Photos** app. This displays the available photos

2. Tap on the **Menu** button at the top of the Photos window to view the options

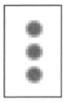

3. Tap on the **Select** button to select one, or more, photo

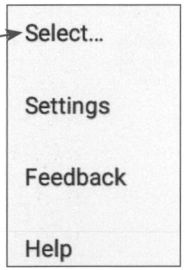

4. Tap on a photo to select it. Use these buttons on the top toolbar to, from left to right, share the album or delete the item

...cont'd

The photos in the Photos app can be worked with and viewed in different ways:

1. Open the **Photos** app

2. Tap on the Photos app **Menu** at the top of the window

3. Tap on the **On device** button to view photos that have been downloaded to your tablet. (Tap on the **Photos** button to view all of your photos, including those stored online by Google)

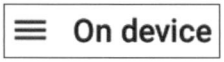

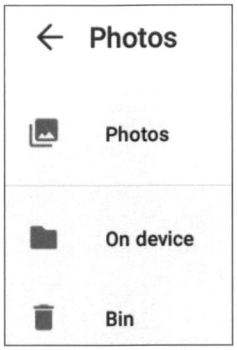

4. The photos are stored in albums according to how they were captured, e.g. **Download** or **Pictures** (for photos taken by the tablet's camera)

5. Tap on the **Menu** button and tap on the **Select** button to select individual photos

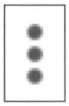

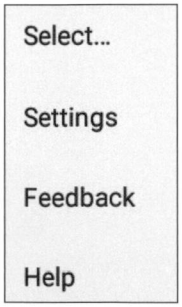

Photos can be added to your Google Account through the **accounts.google.com** website and these will also be available through the Photos app on your tablet, via the **Photos** option in Step 3. To add photos to your Google Account, click on **Google Photos** under **Dashboard** and click on either **Albums** or **Photos** to add more.

6 Tap on individual photos to select them. Tap on the **Menu** button to view the options for working with the selected image(s)

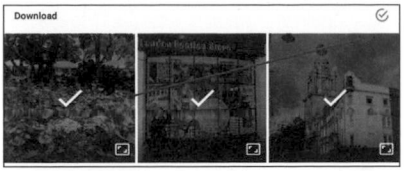

7 Double-tap on a photo to view it at full size

8 Tap on the **Menu** button to view the options for working with the selected full size image. This includes options for displaying the photo's details, printing it, playing a slideshow of all of the images in the current album, setting the photo as a background wallpaper or as an image in your Contacts app, settings for the photo, sending feedback to Google and accessing Help for the Photos app

Details

Print

Slideshow

Set as...

Settings

Feedback

Help

Select the **Set as** option in Step 8 to use the photo as your contact photo for your entry in the **Contacts** app, or as your tablet's background wallpaper.

Editing Photos

Although the Photos app is more for viewing photos, it does have a few editing options so that you can tweak and enhance your images. To access and use these:

1. Open an album, select a single photo and select **Edit photo** from the **Menu** button, or

2. Tap on a photo in an album to view it. Tap on this button to access the editing options

3. For both options above, the photo is displayed in **Edit** mode

Add small editing changes at a time, otherwise the effect may look too severe.

4. Tap on this button to select a pre-set color option from the filmstrip below the photo

5. Additional options for most of the editing functions are displayed on a toolbar below the photo

6. To crop a photo, tap on the **Crop** button and drag the resizing handles as required

7. Tap on this button to **Rotate** the photo manually or left or right

8. Tap on this button to apply preset **Styles** to the photo. These are displayed below the image. Tap on one to apply it

9. Tap on this button to access the saturation option. Drag on the image to alter the saturation levels of color in the image

10. Tap on this button to access the brightness option. Drag on the image to alter the brightness levels in the image

11. Tap on this button to access the exposure option. Drag on the image to alter the overall exposure

12. Drag along the bottom toolbar and use these buttons to apply special effects

13. Press and hold on this button at the top of the window to view the original image as you are applying editing effects

14. Tap on the **Done** button to keep any changes that have been made

Most photos benefit from some cropping, to give the main subject more prominence.

When you edit a photo and save it, a new image is created and the original remains intact.

Sharing Photos

It can be great fun and very rewarding to share photos with friends and family. With an Android tablet this can be done in several ways:

Social networking sites such as Facebook and Twitter are ideal for sharing photos. Their respective apps can be downloaded from the Play Store, in which case they will also appear as one of the sharing options in Step 2.

1. Select an album or open an individual photo and tap on this button on the top toolbar

2. Select one of the sharing options. This will be dependent on the apps on your tablet

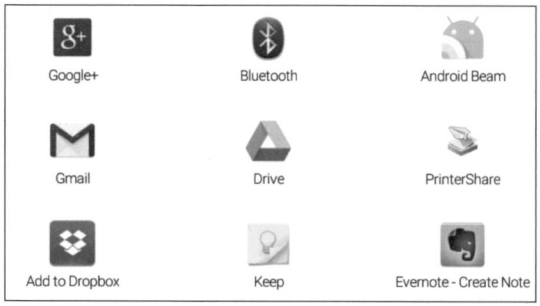

Sharing with Bluetooth

To share with another device with Bluetooth:

If you are sending photos by Bluetooth, the other device must have Bluetooth turned on and accept the request to download the photos when they are sent.

1. Access a photo and tap on the **Bluetooth** button options in Step 2 above

2. If your Bluetooth is not on, tap on the **Turn on** button to activate it

3. Select the device with which you want to share your photo(s). These will be sent wirelessly via Bluetooth

7 Keeping in Touch

This chapter shows how to make the most of different email options, social networking sites, your address book and calendars to keep in touch with people.

134 Email on Android

135 Adding Email Accounts

137 Using Email

139 Email Settings

140 Social Networking

142 Keeping an Address Book

144 Using Your Calendar

146 Using Your Google Account

Email on Android

Email is now a standard feature in most people's digital world. Android tablets provide access to any email accounts that you have. With Android 5.0 and higher the Gmail app is now used for all email services, although two apps are usually still included:

- **Gmail app**. This is the online webmail account provided by Google. When you create a Google Account you will also be provided with a Gmail account. This can be accessed directly from your Android tablet by tapping on the **Gmail** app. It can also be used to link to any of your other email accounts.

- **Email app**. Although this is included with Android 5.0 and higher, it is no longer a functioning email app. If you tap on it you will be informed that it has moved and that the Gmail app will be used for all of your email accounts.

Details of email accounts are displayed under **Accounts** in the **Settings** app. Tap on an email account button to see details of all of the accounts that will be displayed by the **Gmail** app.

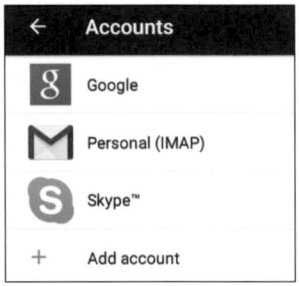

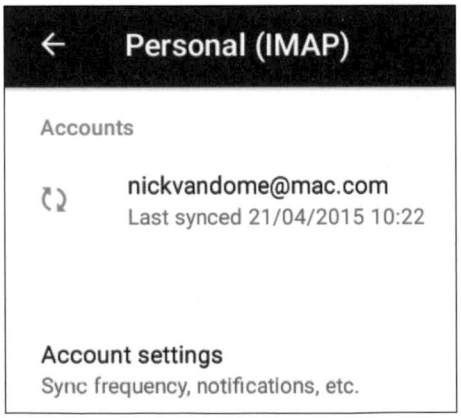

When you view details of email accounts you can also access the account settings for each one, by tapping on the account name.

Adding Email Accounts

Email accounts can be added from the **Accounts** section of the **Settings** app, with the **Add account** button. In addition, they can also be added directly from the Gmail app. To do this:

1. Tap on the **Gmail** app

2. If no account has been added, the Gmail app will open. Tap on the **Add an email address** button

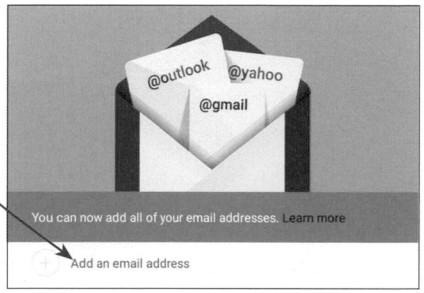

3. Select the type of email account that you want to create and tap on the **OK** button

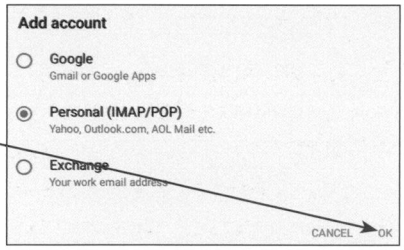

4. Enter your email address and tap on the **Next** button. If the account is not recognized automatically, tap on the **Manual setup** button

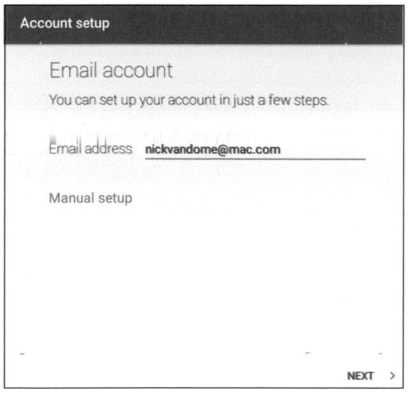

Numerous email accounts can be added to the Gmail app and all of them can be accessed from this single app.

...cont'd

5 For a manual setup, enter the details for the incoming and outgoing email servers. These can be obtained from your email provider. Tap on the **Next** button after each step

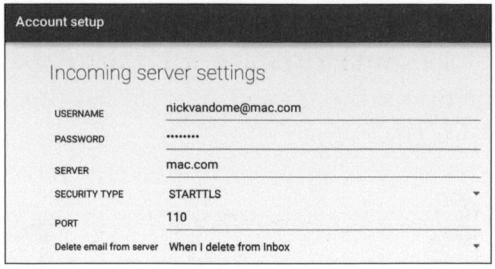

6 After the server settings, select the **Account options** you want to use and tap on the **Next** button

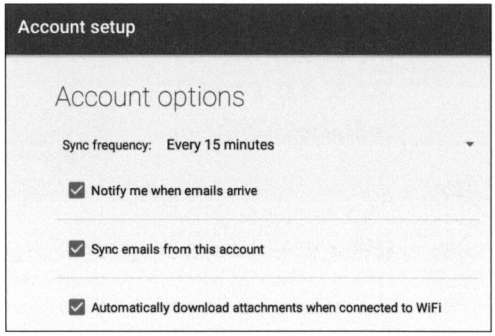

NEXT >

The **Account options** in Step 6 include specifying a notification for when email arrives; syncing email on the server; and automatically downloading email attachments over Wi-Fi.

7 The setup is confirmed. Tap on the **Next** button to open the **Gmail** app and view your messages

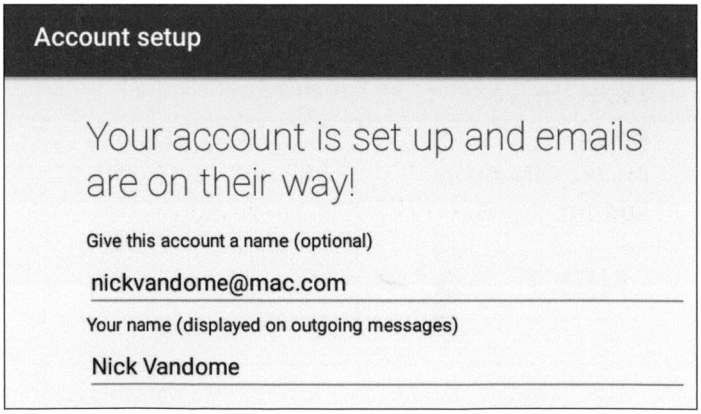

Using Email

Viewing emails

Once you have added email accounts you can view them using the Email app.

1. Tap on the **Gmail** app 

2. Tap here to view the available accounts. Tap on an account to view the messages in it

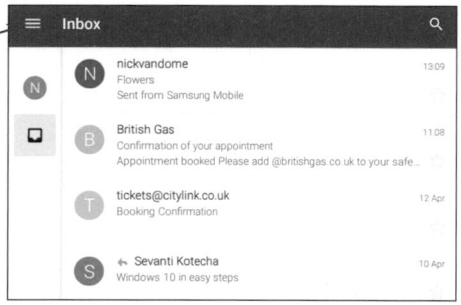

Read messages are displayed with a blue bar next to them on the left-hand side.

3. Tap on the **Inbox** button to view the messages in here

4. Tap on a message to view it. Use these buttons on the top toolbar to, from left to right, delete the email, return to your Inbox, move the email to another folder and access the email's Menu settings

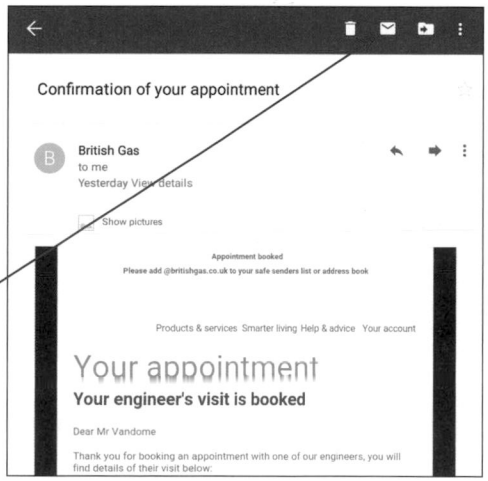

...cont'd

Sending an email

To send an email from the **Email** app:

1. Tap on the **New** button to create a new message

2. A new blank email is created

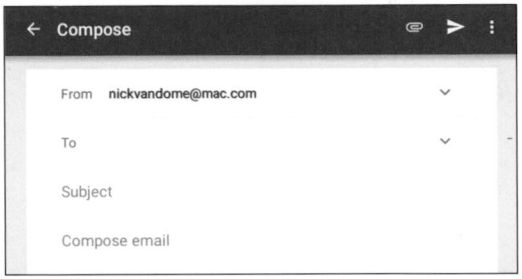

There are no text formatting options in the Email app so you have to use the default text that is supplied.

3. Enter a recipient, a subject and the body text of the email

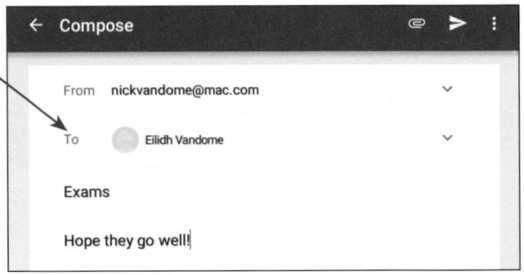

4. Tap on the **Send** button on the top toolbar to send the message

5. Tap on the **Menu** button and tap on the **Save draft** button to keep it and send it at a later date

Email Settings

There are a number of settings that can be applied when using the Email app. They can be accessed from the Email Inbox or when an individual email is being composed.

1. In either the **Inbox** or an individual email, tap on the **Menu** button

2. Tap on the **Settings** button

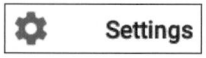

3. Tap on an email account to view its settings

4. All of the settings for the selected account are displayed

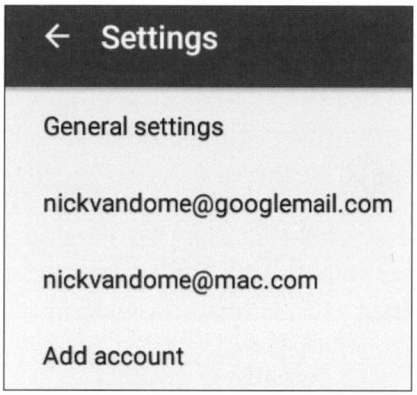

5. Check on the **Notifications** checkbox to enable email notifications to appear in the Notifications area

6. Tap on the **Signature** button to add a message that appears at the end of your emails

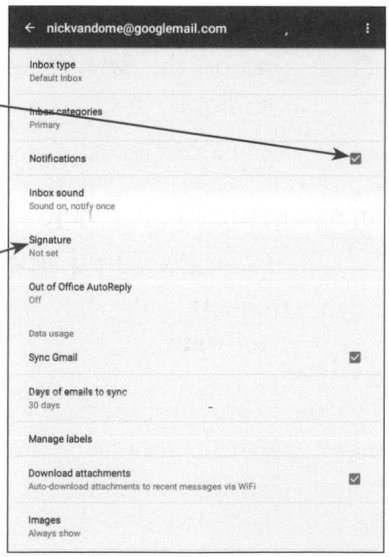

New email accounts can also be added from the main **Settings** screen in Step 3. Tap on the **Add Account** button to do this and follow the requested steps.

Social Networking

Social networking has transformed the way in which we communicate. There are now numerous websites and apps with which we can share information, photos, thoughts, opinions, jokes and almost anything else. Facebook and Twitter have been two of the main players in this area but there is also a range of other sites in the social networking sphere, offering differing options for staying in touch.

On a tablet, the range of social networking sites can be accessed through a web browser or by using the dedicated apps that can be downloaded from the **Play Store**, from within the **Social** category. It is generally better to use the app for a specific social networking site as the interface is well suited to the tablet.

Tap on a social networking app to see details about it and tap on the **Install** button to download it to your tablet.

Some of the most popular social networking sites are:

Google+ is a social networking app that is similar to Facebook in terms of creating online communities for sharing content. It is a built-in app on the Google Nexus and can be accessed from the All Apps area.

Facebook

Despite the range of new sites this is still one of the most widely-used social networking tools. To use Facebook you have to first register, which is free. You can then link up with your friends, and share a variety of content, by searching for them and inviting them with a Friend Request.

Twitter

Twitter is a microblogging site where users post short messages, of up to 140 characters. Once you have joined Twitter, which is free, you can follow other users to see what they are saying and have people follow you too. Messages on Twitter are known as tweets.

Snapchat

Snapchat has quickly caught the imagination of social networking users. It is a messaging service that allows users to send photos and videos to their Snapchat friends, or groups of people. Once these are accessed they remain visible for up to 10 seconds and then they are deleted. Text and graphics can be added to items when they are sent and one of the most frequent uses is for sending self-portraits (selfies). There is the potential for inappropriate material to be sent, and saved, so be careful what you include.

Pinterest

This is an online pinboard, where you can bookmark and 'pin' items of interest and upload your own content for other people to pin. Registration is required for the site, which is free. You can have several of your own pinboards and organize them by subjects and share them with other Pinterest users. You can also add content to your pinboards from websites with the Pinterest button.

Instagram

This is a popular photo and video sharing site. Followers can be added for users and they can then comment and 'like' photos. By default, the security settings are for public viewing of content, so these should be changed if you only want your own followers to be able to view your content.

Tumblr

This combines the functions of a number of other sites and can be used like an online diary, where you post your photos, videos and own thoughts and ideas in a series of blogs. These are known as Tumblelogs and can be viewed by your Tumblr contacts, or everyone if the account is public. If you have Facebook and Twitter accounts your Tumblr content can also be linked to these. It can be harder to make your account private on Tumblr than on some other sites.

YouTube is one of the great successes of the Internet age. It is a video sharing site, with millions of video clips covering every subject imaginable. There is a built-in YouTube app on most Android tablets, which can be accessed from the All Apps button.

Keeping an Address Book

An important part of staying in touch with people is having an up-to-date address book. On an Android tablet this can be done with the **Contacts** app:

Some tablets have their own default address book and calendar apps, which can be used in a similar way to the ones shown on the following pages. The Contacts app and the Calendar app can be downloaded from the Play Store and these are the best ones to use if you want to sync your items with your Google Account.

1. Tap on the **Contacts** app

2. Your own basic details are already included from when you first set up your tablet

3. Tap on the **Edit** button to add more details to your own entry

4. Tap here and enter more information about your contact details

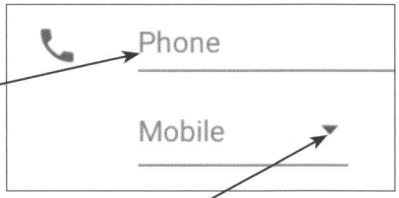

5. Tap here on one of the items to view additional options

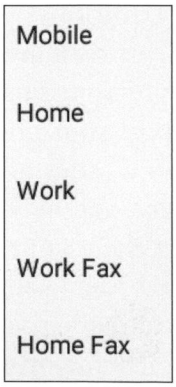

Entries in the Contacts app are also available online in your Google Account. This means that you can access them whenever you are online on another computer.

6 Tap here and take a photo with the tablet's camera or select one from the **Photos** app. This will be your profile picture

7 Tap on the **Edit contact** button to go back to the contact's main page

Adding contacts

To add more people to your address book in the **Contacts** app:

1 Tap on the **New** button to add a new contact

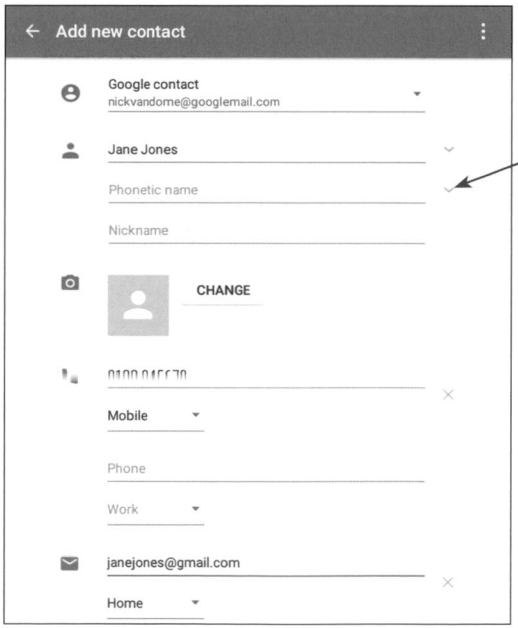

Tap on the arrow next to a field to access more options for that item.

2 Enter the details of the new contact

Using Your Calendar

The Calendar app can be used to add items such as events, meetings and birthdays. You can use these on your tablet and they will also be available online from any Internet-enabled computer or mobile device via your Google Account. To use the Calendar:

A range of national and public holidays are pre-inserted into your calendar, usually based on your location.

1. Tap on the **Calendar** app

2. The calendar is displayed and the view can be customized in a number of ways

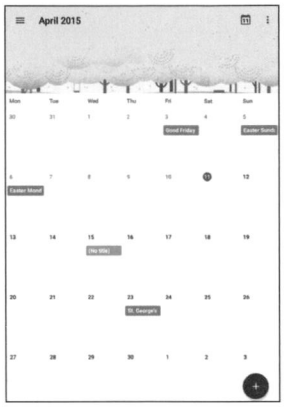

3. Tap on this button to view the current day at any point

4. Tap on the **Menu** button at the top of the window to view the calendar by day, week or month or to display all of the events that have been added

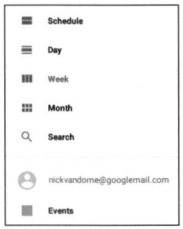

5. Swipe left and right on the main calendar to view different days, weeks and months. Tap on a day to go to that point

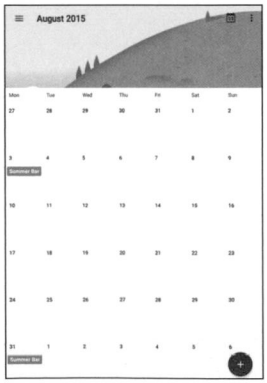

Adding events

One of the main uses for the calendar is adding events:

1. In Day or Week view, tap and hold on a time slot and tap on the **Tap to create** window, or

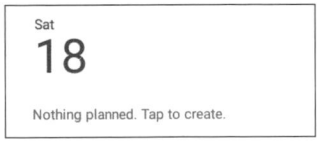

2. In any view, tap on this button to add a new event

3. The event will be linked to your Google Account email address

4. Enter the details for the event including: what, where, from, to and a description

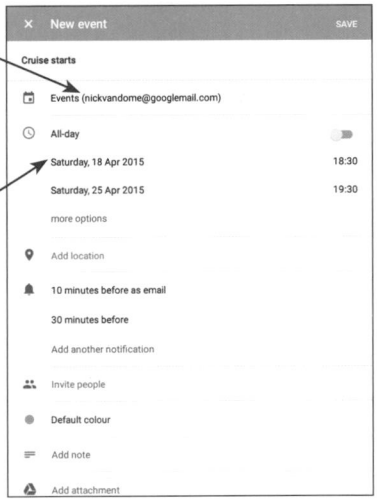

5. Tap on the **Does not repeat** button if it is a recurring event and select the frequency

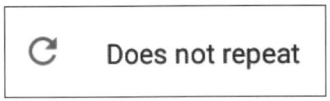

6. Tap here to select a time for a reminder for the event

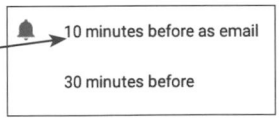

7. Tap on the **Save** button to add the event

The Calendar is linked to your Google Account and events will be displayed here if you access your Calendar at **accounts.google.com**

Recurring events can be used for items such as birthdays.

Using Your Google Account

When you have a Google Account, the information that you enter into your communication apps such as Gmail, Calendar and Contacts can also be viewed online whenever you are logged in to your account. To do this:

1. Tap on your Google account details under **Settings > Accounts**

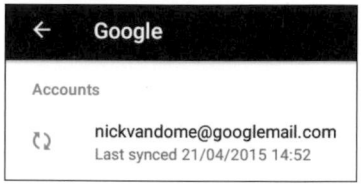

2. Ensure that the sync options are On

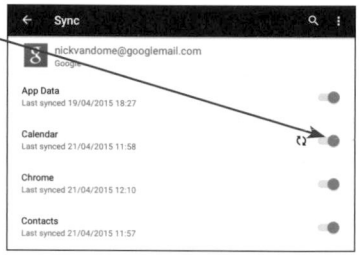

3. Log in to your Google Account online at **accounts.google.com** and tap on the **Dashboard** button

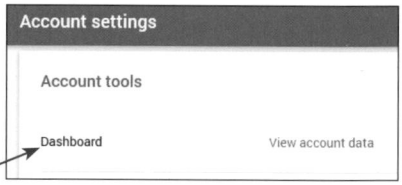

4. Tap on one of the relevant services to view the information from your Android app that has been synced with your Google Account, such as the Calendar. The details should be the same as for the item on your tablet

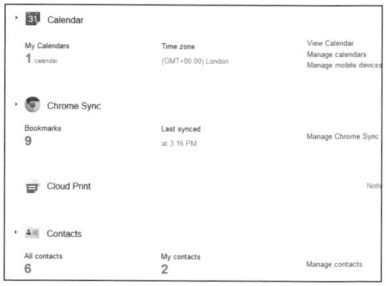

To view the information from your Contacts app through your online Google Account, click on the **Dashboard** link and click on the **Contacts** option.

8 Browsing the Web

This chapter looks at browser options on Android and also using all of your favorite websites with the default Chrome browser.

148 Android Web Browsers

149 Opening Pages

150 Bookmarking Pages

152 Links and Images

153 Using Tabs

154 Being Incognito

155 Browser Settings

Android Web Browsers

Web browsing is an essential part of our digital world and on Android tablets this functionality is provided by a variety of web browsers customized for this purpose. They can usually display websites in two ways:

- Optimized for viewing on mobile devices, which are versions that are designed specifically for viewing in this format.
- Full versions of websites, rather than the mobile versions, which are the same as used on a desktop computer.

Mobile versions of a website usually have **m.** before the rest of the website address, e.g. **m.mysite.com**

Different Android tablets have different default browsers but they all have the same general functionality:

- Viewing web pages.
- Bookmarking pages.
- Tabbed browsing, i.e. using tabs to view more than one web page within the same browser window.

If you do not want to use the default browser that is provided with your tablet, there is a range of browsers that can be downloaded, for free, from the Play Store.

Enter **browsers for android** into the **Play Store Search box** to view the available options.

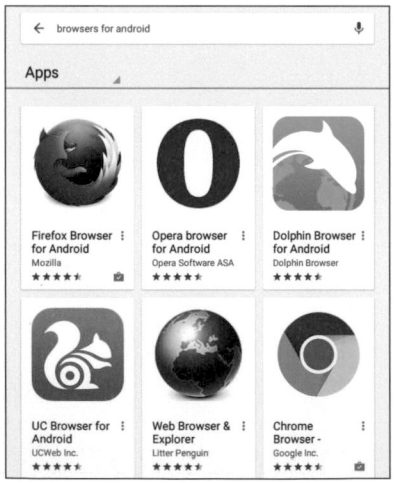

Opening Pages

Web pages can be opened on a tablet in an almost identical way as on a desktop computer or laptop. For some Android web browsers, there is a list of top sites when you open a browser or create a new tab. (The examples on the following pages are for the **Chrome** browser but other browsers operate in a similar way.)

1. When you first open Chrome, the **Search/ Address** box at the top of the page can be used to search for keywords or phrases, or you can use it to find specific web pages and sites. Enter text into the **Search/Address** box

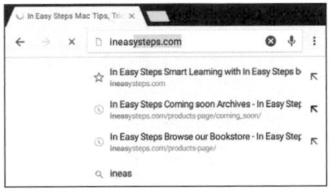

2. Tap on an item with this icon to go to a web page. Tap on one to go to a list of results or tap on one to go to that website

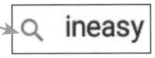

3. Tap on an item with this icon to go a web page with the search results for the item

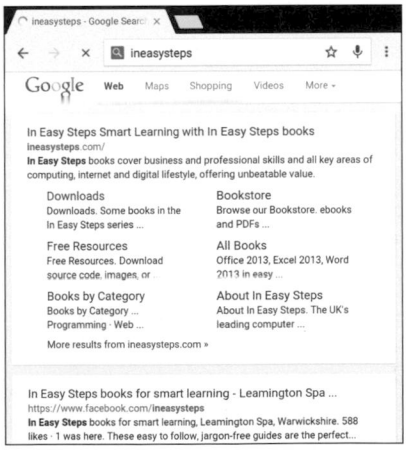

The Chrome browser can be downloaded from the Play Store if it is not already on your tablet. This is a Google product and integrates closely with other Google apps on your tablet.

Swipe outwards with your thumb and forefinger on a web page to zoom in on it; pinch inwards to zoom back out. Double-tap with one finger to zoom in and out too, but this zooms in to a lesser degree than swiping.

Bookmarking Pages

The favorite pages that you visit can be bookmarked so that you can find them quickly. To do this:

1. Open the page that you want to bookmark and tap on the star button in the **Search/ Address** box

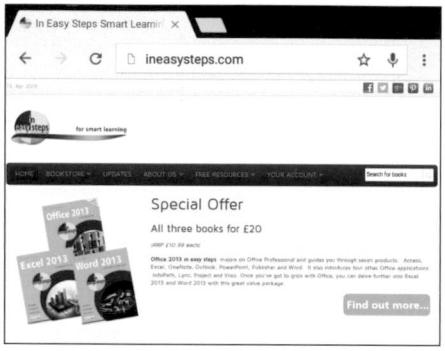

2. Tap in the **Name** box and enter a name for the bookmark

3. Tap in the **Folder** box to specify a folder into which you want to save the bookmark

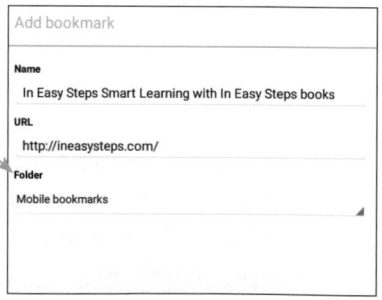

If bookmarks are saved into the **Mobile Bookmarks** folder they will also be available on other mobile devices.

4. Tap on a folder to select it, or tap on the **New folder** button to create a new folder to use

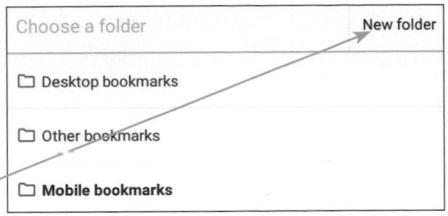

5. Tap on the **Save** button in the **Add bookmark** window to save the bookmarked web page

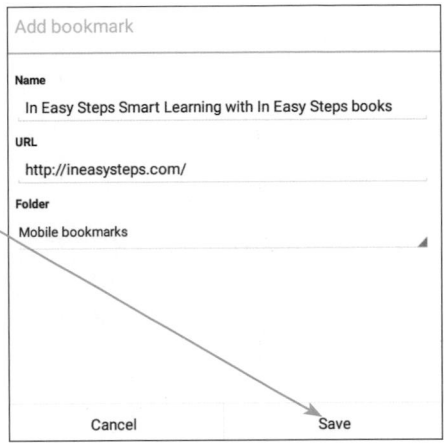

6. The star button turns blue which indicates the page is bookmarked

The **Menu** button can also be used to open a new tab. See page 153 for more details.

Viewing bookmarks

To view pages that have been bookmarked:

1. To view bookmarks, tap on the **Menu** button and tap on the **Bookmarks** button

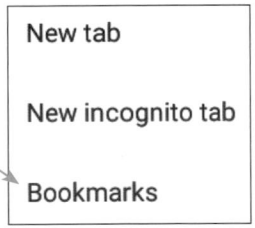

2. The bookmarked pages are displayed in their relevant folders. Tap on one to open that page

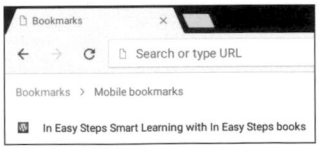

Links and Images

Links and images are both essential items on websites; links provide the functionality for moving between pages and sites, while images provide the all-important graphical element. To work with these:

If you use the **Save link** option for a link, the page will be downloaded and available from the **Downloads** app in the **All Apps** section. This will enable you to view the content when you are offline.

1. Tap and hold on a link to access its menu (tap once on a link to go directly to the linked page). The options on the menu are for opening the link in a new tab, opening it in a new tab that does not get recorded by the browser's history (**Open in incognito tab**), copying it so that it could be emailed to someone, and saving the linked page as a download so that it can be viewed offline

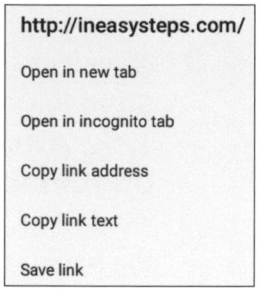

2. Tap and hold on an image to access its menu. The options are for saving it (into the Gallery app), viewing it on its own on the current page (**Open image**) and opening the image in a new tab. For both of the latter two options the image is displayed on its own on a page

Using Tabs

Tabs are now a common feature on web browsers and are a function whereby you can open numerous pages within the same browser window. To do this:

1. Tap on this button at the top right-hand corner of the browser window to add a new tab, or

2. Tap on the **Menu** button and tap on the **New tab** button

3. Open a new page from the **Bookmarks** folder or by entering a web address or search word into the **Search/ Address** box

4. New tabs are opened at the top of the browser. Tap on the tab heading to move to that page

5. If too many tabs are opened for the available space on the screen, they are stacked on top of each other

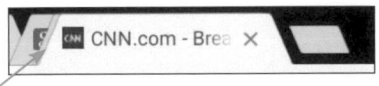

6. Tap on the cross on a tab to close it

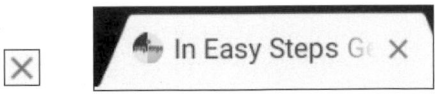

If there are a lot of tabs open, swipe left and right on the tabs bar to move between them all.

Being Incognito

If you do not want a record to be kept of the web pages that you have visited, most browsers have a function where you can view pages 'in private' so that the details are not stored by the browser. In Chrome this is performed with the Incognito function:

If the Incognito option is used, web pages will not be stored in the browser history or the search history.

1. Tap on the **Menu** button and tap on the **New incognito tab** button

New tab

New incognito tab

2. The incognito page opens in a new tab, but any other open tabs are not visible (unless they are incognito too). Open a web page in the same way as for a standard tab

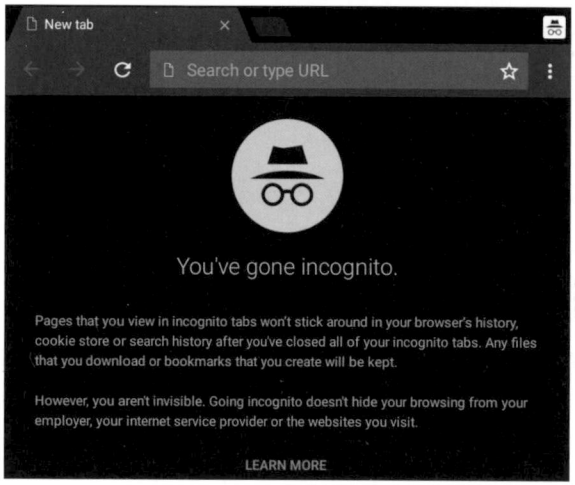

3. Incognito pages are denoted by this icon at the top left-hand corner of the browser

4. Tap on this button to toggle between incognito tabs and standard tabs. In each view, the tabs in the other view are not visible

If children are using your tablet then you may not know what they are looking at on the Web if they use the Incognito option. See page 176 for details about restricting access to apps on your tablet, using the restricted profile option.

Browser Settings

Mobile browsers have the usual range of settings that can be accessed from the **Menu** button.

1. Tap on the **Menu** button and tap on the **Settings** button

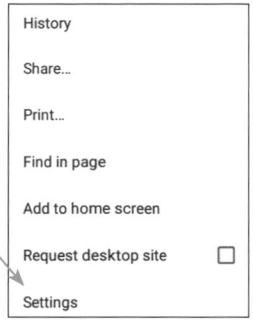

Some of the Settings include:

- **Search engine**. This can be used to set a default search engine for the browser.

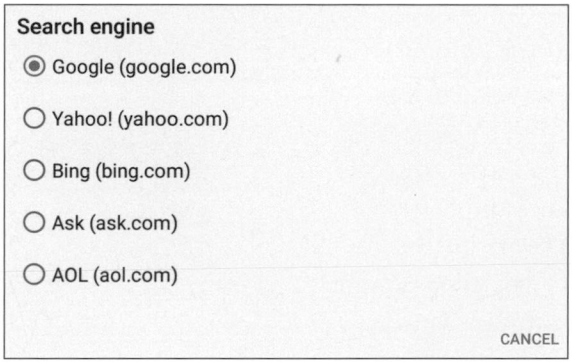

- **Auto-fill forms**. Use this to make selections for how online forms are dealt with by the browser.

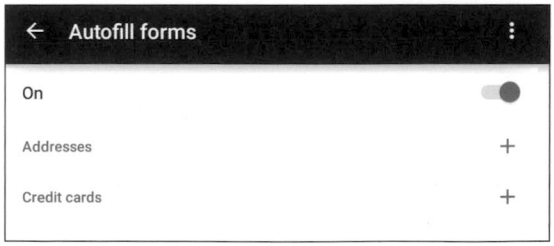

If other people are going to be using your account on your tablet do not turn on auto-fill options for credit or debit cards. If other people are using the tablet, it is best to set up individual accounts for them; see pages 172-173 for details.

...cont'd

- Under the **Advanced** heading, tap on the **Privacy** button to specify how your browsing data is used.

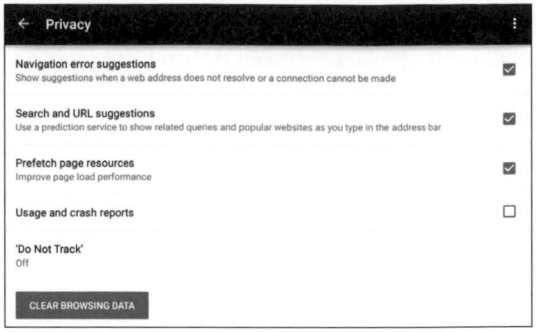

A cookie is a small piece of data that is stored by the browser containing information about websites that have been visited.

- Under the **Advanced** heading, tap on the **Accessibility** button to specify the text size for viewing web pages.

- Under the **Advanced** heading, tap on the **Site settings** button. Check on or off the options for cookies, JavaScript (which is required to give you full functionality of most websites) and pop-up menus. Tap on the **Location** button to specify whether Google apps can use your current location and the **All sites** button to view settings for individual websites.

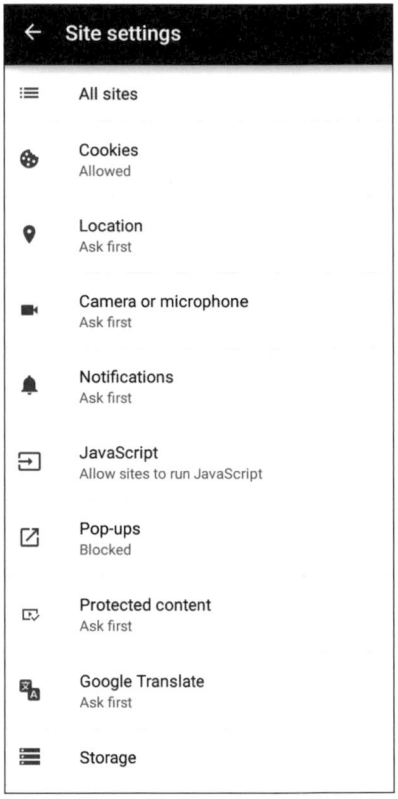

- Under the **Advanced** heading, tap on the **Data Saver** button to specify how web pages are pre-loaded.

9 On Your Travels

Tablets are an ideal traveling companion and this chapter looks at some of the issues connected with this.

158 Traveling with Your Tablet

160 Keeping Your Tablet Safe

161 Airport Security

162 Finding Hotels and Flights

164 Calling with Skype

166 Useful Travel Apps

Traveling with Your Tablet

When you go traveling there are a few essentials that you have to consider: passport, money and insurance, to name three. To this you can add your tablet; it is a perfect traveling companion that can help you plan your trip and keep you informed and entertained when you are away from home.

Social networking sites can be a great asset when you are traveling: you can keep in touch with family and friends and post your photos and videos as soon as you have taken them so that people can see them even before you get home.

Uses for traveling

There are a lot of Play Store apps that can be used for different aspects of traveling. However, the built-in apps can also be put to good use before and during your travels:

- **Maps**. Use this for accessing maps of your destinations, finding directions and viewing images of areas to which you are traveling.

- **Contacts**. Keep your Contacts app address book up-to-date so that you can use it to send postcards to friends and family and access contact details.

- **Gmail**. With a Wi-Fi connection on holiday you can keep in touch with everyone through the Gmail app and also send them photos of your trip.

- **Play Music**. Use this app to play your favorite music while you are traveling or relaxing at your destination.

- **Photos**. Store photos of your trip with this app and play them back as a slideshow when you get back home.

- **Calculator**. Use this to work out the cost of items by converting prices from the local currency. Use it in conjunction with a currency converter for best results.

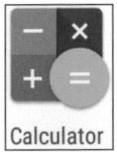

- **Play Books** (and **Play Newsstand**). Instead of dragging lots of heavy books around, use this app for your holiday library.

Using Google Now on your travels

As shown on pages 52-56, Google Now can be used to display cards with a range of realtime information. When you are traveling this can be an excellent way to keep informed about your location. The Google Now cards that can be used for this include:

- **Travel**. This card is dependent on your geographical location. If it is turned on, your tablet's location-based services will determine your location in the world and provide information accordingly in Google Now. This includes local currency, translation options, the time back home and information about local attractions.

- **Photo spot nearby**. This card can be used to display good photo opportunities when you are out and about. An active Internet connection is required for this so that location-based services can identify where you are and locate the nearest popular photo spots that are identified by Google.

- **Public transport**. When you are near to bus or train stations this card will appear with details of available public transport. The options are for showing the card when around train stations, bus stops or when traveling anywhere. However, you will probably need mobile Internet access in the form of a 3G or 4G service, unless there is public Wi-Fi available near to the public transport station.

- **Places**. This card can be used to show places of interest when you are in a town or city. The options are for showing the card with relevant items when near to restaurants/bars, museums and shops.

For the Google Now cards used when traveling, a Wi-Fi or 3G/4G connection is required so that you can connect to the Internet to get the relevant information.

Keeping Your Tablet Safe

By most measures, tablets are valuable items. However, in a lot of countries around the world their relative value can be a lot more than it is to their owners; in some countries the value of a tablet could easily equate to several months' wages. Even in countries where their relative value is not so high they can still be seen as a lucrative opportunity for thieves. Therefore, it is important to try to keep your tablet as safe as possible when you are on vacation. Some points to consider in relation to this are:

- If possible, try to keep your tablet with you at all times, i.e. transport it in a piece of luggage that you can carry rather than having to put it into a large case.
- Never hand over your tablet, or any other of your belongings, to anyone who promises to look after them.
- If you do have to detach yourself from your tablet, try to put it somewhere secure, such as a hotel safe.
- When you are traveling, try to keep your tablet as unobtrusive as possible. This is where a small backpack can prove useful, as it is not immediately apparent that you are carrying a tablet.
- Do not use your tablet in areas where you think it may attract undue interest from the locals, particularly in obviously poor areas. For instance, if you are in a local café the appearance of a tablet may create unwanted attention for you. If in doubt, wait until you get back to your hotel.
- If you are accosted by criminals who demand your tablet then hand it over. No piece of equipment is worth suffering physical injury for.
- Make sure your tablet is covered by your vacation insurance. If not, get separate insurance for it.
- Trust your instincts with your tablet. If something doesn't feel right, then don't do it.

Before you leave on vacation, make sure that your tablet is backed up, using the **Backup & reset** option in the **Personal** section of the **Settings** app. Drag the **Back up my data** button On.

Airport Security

Because of the increased global security following terrorist attacks throughout the beginning of the 21st century, the levels of airport security have been greatly increased around the world. This has implications for all travelers, and if you are traveling with a tablet this may add to the security scrutiny which you will face. When dealing with airport security when traveling with a tablet there are some issues that you should always keep in mind:

- Keep your tablet with you at all times. Unguarded baggage at airports immediately raises suspicion and it can make life very easy for thieves.
- Carry your tablet in a small bag so that you can take it on board as hand luggage. On no account should it be put in with your luggage that goes in the hold.
- X-ray machines at airports will not harm your tablet. However, if anyone tries to scan it with a metal detector, ask them if they can inspect it by hand instead.
- Keep a careful eye on your tablet when it goes through the X-ray conveyor belt and try to be there at the other side as soon as it emerges. In some countries there have been stories of people causing a commotion at the security gate just after someone has placed electronic devices on the conveyor belt. While everyone's attention (including yours) is distracted, an accomplice takes the device from the conveyor belt. If you are worried about this you can ask for the security guard to hand-check your tablet rather than putting it on the conveyor belt.
- Make sure the battery of your tablet is fully charged. This is because you may be asked to turn on your tablet to verify that it is just that, and not some other device disguised as a tablet.
- When you are on the plane, keep the tablet in the storage area under your seat, rather than in the overhead locker, so that you know where it is at all times.

If you put your tablet in your main luggage there is a chance that it could be taken out of it when it is being loaded onto the plane.

Finding Hotels and Flights

The Play Store is an excellent vehicle for finding good value hotel rooms and flights around the world. When hotels have spare capacity, this can quickly be relayed to associated websites, where users can usually benefit from cheap prices and special offers. There are plenty of apps that have details of thousands of hotels around the world, such as:

TripAdvisor

One of the top travel apps, this not only has hotel information but also restaurants, activities and flights. Enter a destination in the Search box and then navigate through the available options.

Hotels.com

A stylish app that enables you to enter search keywords or find local hotels depending on your current location. You can also view any reservations that you have made.

If you are booking hotel rooms, look at several apps as some of them have the same rooms, but at different prices from each other.

Booking.com

Another good, fully featured hotel app that provides a comprehensive service and excellent prices.

LateRooms.com

An app that specializes in getting the best prices by dealing with rooms that are available at short notice. Some genuine bargains can be found here, for hotels of all categories.

Trivago

Another app for finding good value hotel rooms around the world. Hotels can be viewed according to location and then filtered according to popularity, rating, price, number of stars and distance from your location.

Orbitz

A comprehensive travel app that covers flights, hotels and car rentals. It can also be used to enter details about your itinerary, although you need to sign in for this.

Kayak

Another all-round travel app that enables you to book flights, hotels and cars. You can also view your itinerary and there is a flight tracker function too.

Expedia Hotels & Flights

The mobile app for the popular online travel company, where you can book all of your travel requirements by entering your destination and dates of travel.

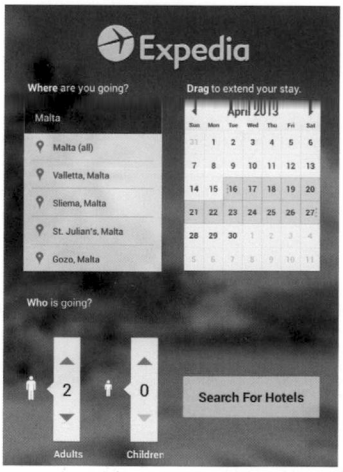

Calling with Skype

Just because you are on vacation does not mean that you cannot keep in touch with family and friends at home, and calls with the Skype app via your tablet are an ideal way to do this. As long as you have Wi-Fi access to the Internet you can make voice and video calls to other Skype users, free of charge. To use Skype:

Skype voice and video calls are free to other Skype users. Calls to non-Skype users have to be paid for.

1. Access the **Play Store** and download the Skype app

2. Open **Skype** by tapping on this button

3. If you already have a Skype account, enter your details, or tap on the **Create account** button to create a new account

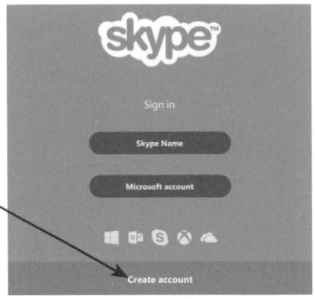

4. Your contacts are displayed under **People** on the Homepage

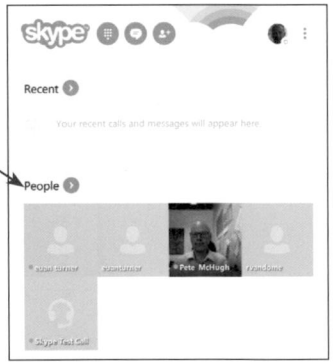

5. Tap on a contact to view their details and contact them by voice or video with these buttons at the top of the window, or by instant messaging with the text box at the bottom of the window

Adding Skype contacts

To add new contacts to call in Skype:

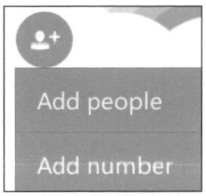

1. Tap here and tap on either **Add people** or **Add number**

2. Tap on the **Find people on Skype** button

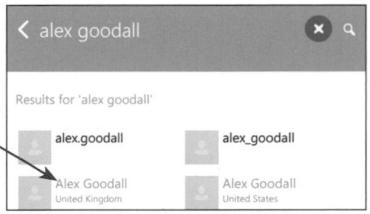

3. Enter a name into the Search box and tap on one of the results

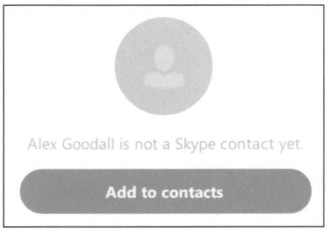

4. Matches for the requested person are shown. Tap on a person's name and tap on the **Add to contacts** button to send a contact request

5. The selected person will then be sent a Skype request and they have to accept it before they become a full contact. Enter the text you want to use for the request, or use the default text that is pre-inserted

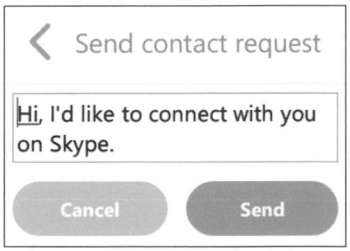

6. Tap on the **Send** button to send the message and request that the person accepts you as a contact

Once you add the Skype app to your tablet your Skype contacts will also be available in your **Contacts** app.

Calls can also be made directly to numbers, using the keypad. Tap on this button on the main toolbar to access the Skype keypad.

Useful Travel Apps

In addition to hotel and flight apps there are also numerous apps from the Play Store that can be used for several areas of planning and organizing your trip. Some to look at are:

City Guides and Maps

Enter the name of a major city around the world (New York, London, Paris, Sydney etc.) into the Play Store Search box and you will be presented with a list of results for city guides, maps and transit details for the selected city.

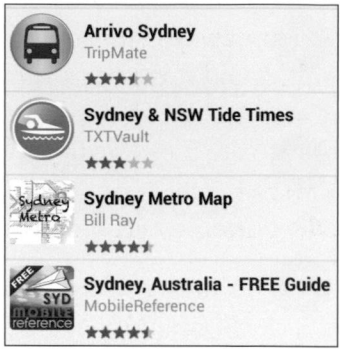

TripAdvisor City Guides

As above, these are some of the most comprehensive city guides in the Play Store. They include a wide range of information, from restaurants, hotels, attractions, transport and tours, to nightlife and shopping. It also includes reviews and comments from people who have visited the restaurants and sights listed in the app.

If you visit somewhere recommended in an app such as TripAdvisor, post a review to help give other people more information about it.

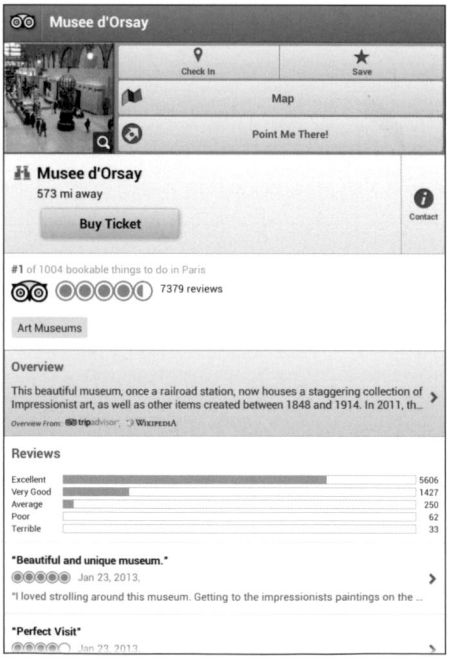

Wi-Fi Finder

Using Wi-Fi for accessing the Internet and the range of Google services on your tablet is an essential function when using your device at home, and it is just as important when you are away from home. This app locates Wi-Fi access points and hotspots around your current location and there is also an offline database that lists Wi-Fi hotspots around the world. Tap on the **Wi-Fi Scanner** button to find all Wi-Fi points near you and tap on the **Public Wi-Fi Near Me** button to view all of the public Wi-Fi points nearby.

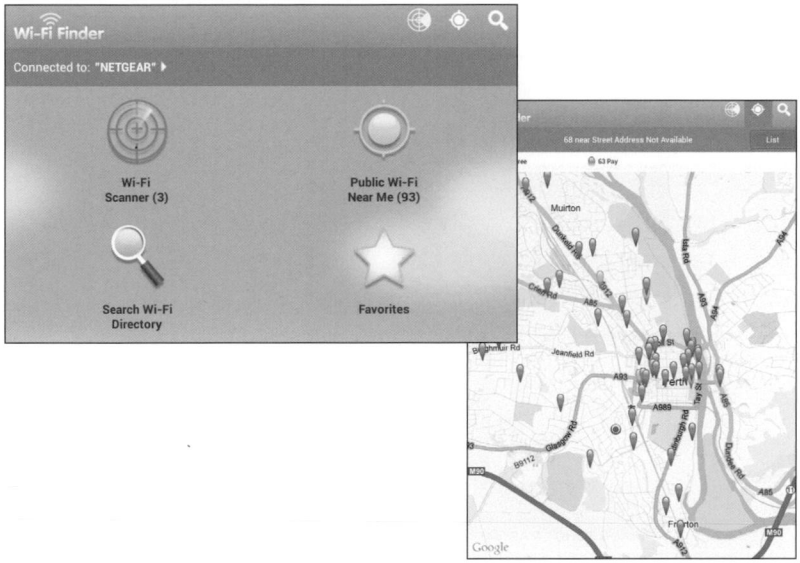

If you are traveling somewhere, look up the Wi-Fi hotspots before you leave, as you will not be able to use the app if you are not already connected to Wi-Fi, although you can still use the offline database if you have downloaded it.

World Atlas

A basic atlas that can help you plan your trip and find countries around the world. Swipe to move around the globe and pinch outwards with thumb and forefinger to zoom in on an area. Pinch inwards to zoom back out again.

...cont'd

My World Heritage Passport

The UNESCO World Heritage sites offer some of the most stunning and interesting locations around the world. This app enables you to view them by a variety of criteria and also view a range of information about each site.

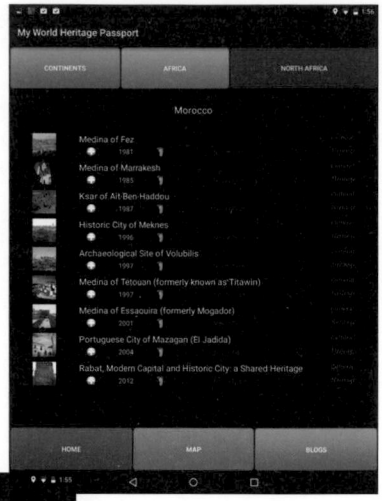

Look up the UNESCO World Heritage website at **whc.unesco.org** for detailed information about these fascinating and diverse areas.

XE Currency

This app delivers information about exchange rates for all major world currencies and also a wealth of background information such as high and low rates and historical charts.

10 Sharing with the Family

This chapter shows how best to give safe access to other family members and guest users.

170 About Multiple Users

172 Adding Family Members

174 Switching Between Users

175 Guest Users

176 Restricted Profiles

About Multiple Users

Because of the power and flexibility that is available in a tablet computer, it seems a waste to restrict it to a single user. One way to do this is simply to let different people use the tablet whenever they have access to it. However, since everyone likes their own music, books and movies, and different people use different types of apps, it makes much more sense to allow people to set up their individual user accounts. This creates their own personal area that can be protected from anyone else accessing it.

Not all tablets allow for multiple users, but with some versions of Android (4.2 and later) it is possible to add multiple users on a tablet. This means that they have their own private space on the tablet where they can access their own content and apply the settings that they want. Each separate account can also be protected by its own password. Once accounts have been set up, they can be accessed from the buttons at the top right-hand corner of the Notifications screen. Tap on a current user to view the other options.

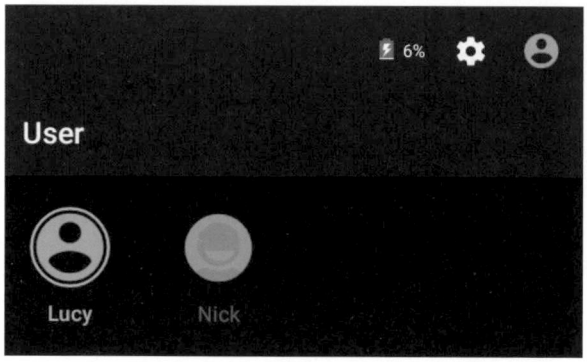

Without user accounts, the tablet will automatically display the default account. However, if different user accounts have been set up on the tablet, a list of these accounts will be displayed in the Notifications Area.

The relevant user can then tap on their own account to access it. At this point they can enter their password (or swipe the lock button) to gain access to their own account.

Customization

Once individual accounts have been set up, it is possible for each individual user to customize their account, i.e. to set the way in which their account appears and operates. This means that each user can apply their own settings, such as the appearance of the Home screen:

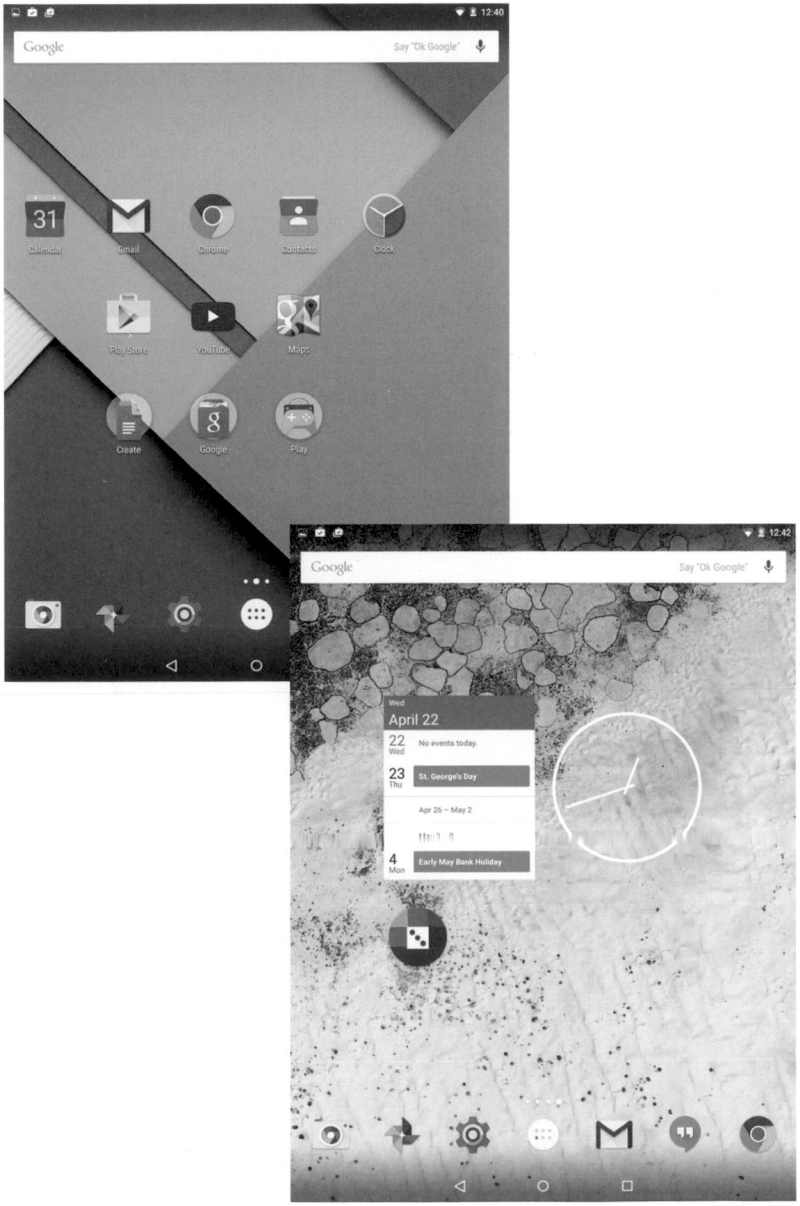

When other users are logged in to their own account you will not be able to control what they are using or looking at in terms of apps and content, unless it is a restricted profile; see page 176.

Adding Family Members

The person who first sets up the tablet is the owner of it and they have ultimate control in terms of adding and deleting other users. To add a new user:

1. Tap on the **All Apps** button

2. Tap on the **Settings** app

3. Under the **Device** section, tap on the **Users** button

4. Your information is displayed as the current user, and owner, of the tablet. Tap on the **Add user or profile** button

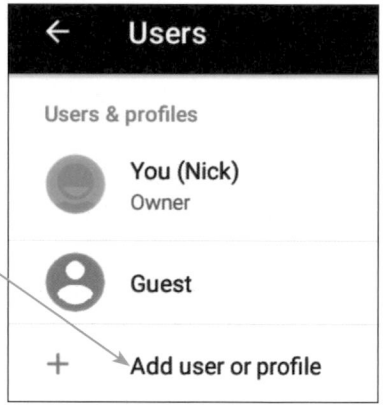

New users have to create a Google Account in order to use and authenticate their own account on the tablet.

5. Select whether you want the new user to have a restricted profile or not (e.g. for children)

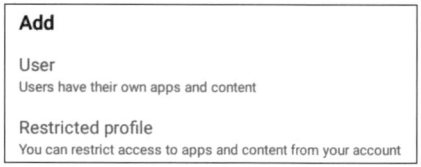

6. Tap on the **OK** button to add the new user

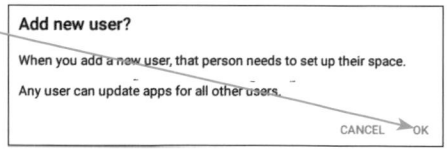

7. Tap on the **Set up now** button (the new user will now have to enter their details)

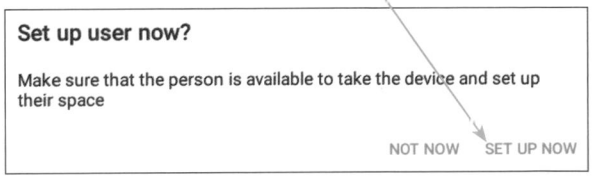

8. Once the new user has been added, their user's icon will be displayed at the top of the Lock Screen when they are using their account

9. Swipe the padlock icon to the edge of the circle to unlock the screen for the new user, or enter a password or PIN if this is how the Lock Screen has been set up

10. The **Welcome** screen notifies you that you have been added as a new user on the tablet. Tap on the arrow to move through the setup process. This is similar to creating a user when the tablet is first set up. The new user will also have to create a Google Account

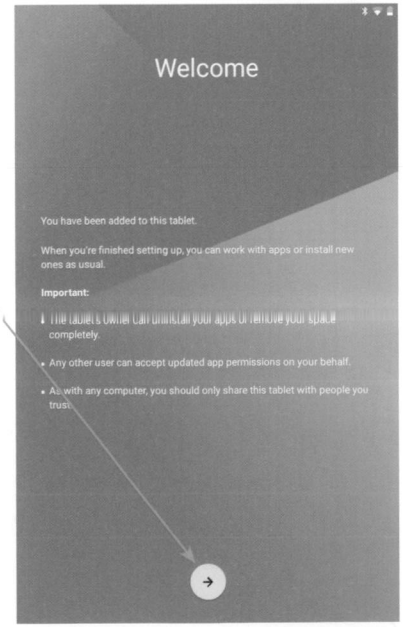

Each individual user can set a password that has to be entered to unlock the tablet for access to their own content. For more details about this, see pages 46-47.

Switching Between Users

It is possible to switch between users from either the Lock Screen or the Quick Settings.

From the Lock Screen

New users can also be added from Step 2. To do this, tap on the **Add user** button.

1. From the Lock Screen, tap on the icon for the current user at the top of the screen

2. Tap on another user's icon

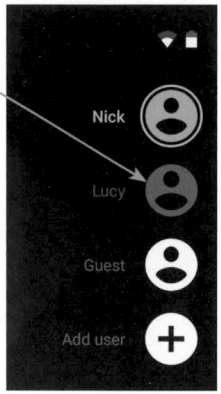

3. The new user's icon is displayed at the top of the Lock Screen

From the Quick Settings

The most secure way to lock your tablet is with a password, using upper and lower case letters, numbers and symbols.

1. Swipe down from the top of the screen to access the Quick Settings. Tap on a user's icon and then tap on it again to view other users. Tap on one to make that the active account

Guest Users

As well as being able to add new users to your tablet, you can also add guest users (with Android 5.0 and above). This can be useful for someone who wants to use your tablet on a single occasion, without the need for a permanent account. To set up a guest user:

1. From the Lock Screen, tap on the current user and tap on the **Add guest** button or, do the same from the Quick Settings by dragging down from the top of the screen

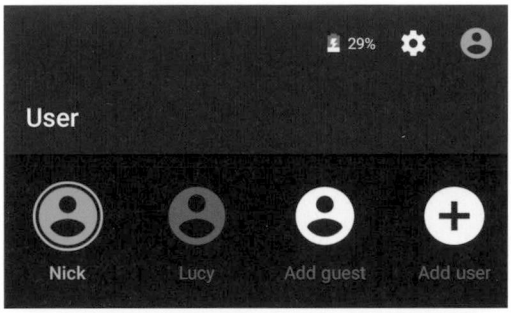

2. The **Guest** icon is displayed on the guest's Lock Screen and can also be accessed from the Quick Settings section

3. Tap on the Guest button and tap on the **Remove guest** button to delete the current guest account. Subsequent guest accounts can be set up after another guest account has been removed

If you let a guest user have access to your tablet, make sure that you lock your own account with a PIN or a password.

Restricted Profiles

Tablets are great devices for children and grandchildren; their portability and range of apps can make them the ideal device for playing games, watching videos and communicating with friends. However, these same benefits can also be a disadvantage as far as parents and grandparents are concerned, as you may not always be able to see what your children are doing on the tablet as they may be in a different place from you. One option for this is to set up a new user with a restricted profile where you can specify which apps they are unable to use. To do this:

A range of parental control apps can also be downloaded from the Play Store, which can be used to restrict access to content, or allow access to specific apps. Some to look at include: Kids Place, Funamo, Net Nanny and Norton Family.

1. Follow the process for adding a new user as shown on page 172. Instead of adding a standard user, tap on the **Restricted profile** button

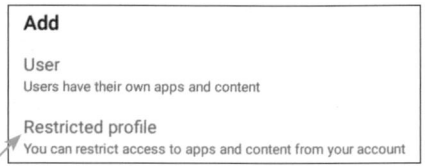

2. Drag the buttons On for the items you want included for the user

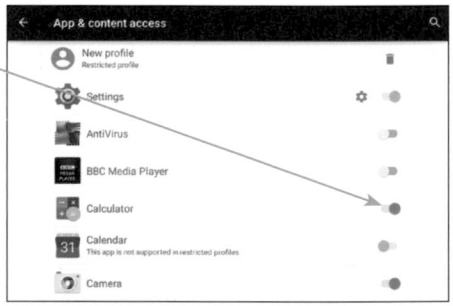

3. Only the selected apps are available to the user with the restricted profile

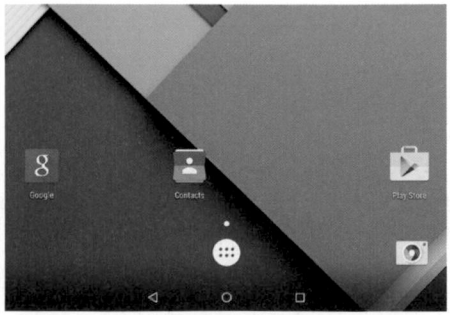

11 Accessibility and Security

This chapter looks at security issues with antivirus apps and finding a lost tablet.

178 Accessibility

180 Security Issues

181 About Antivirus Apps

182 Using Antivirus Apps

184 Locating Your Tablet

Accessibility

It is important for tablets to be accessible for as wide a range of users as possible, including those with visual or physical and motor issues. In Android this is done through the **Accessibility** settings. To use these:

1. Tap on the **Settings** app

2. Under the **System** section, tap on the **Accessibility** button

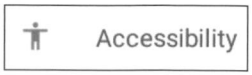

3. Tap on an item to turn it On or Off, or check on these boxes to enable functionality for increasing the text size, auto-rotating the screen and having passwords spoken as they are entered

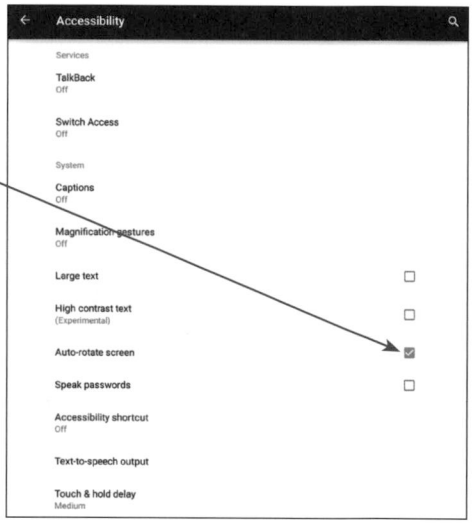

4. Tap on the **TalkBack** button in Step 3 and drag this button to **On** to activate TalkBack, whereby the tablet will provide spoken information about items on screen and those which are being accessed

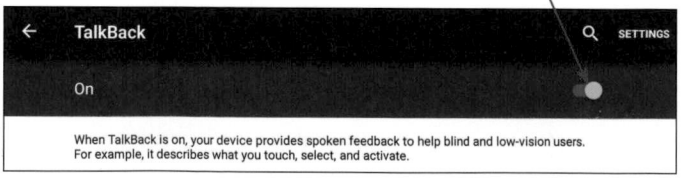

If you check On the **Large text** option, this will increase the text size for the system text on your tablet, but not necessarily the text in your apps, unless they have this functionality.

5 TalkBack also provides an **Explore by Touch** function that enhances TalkBack by providing an audio description of what is on the screen. Tap on the **OK** button to activate TalkBack

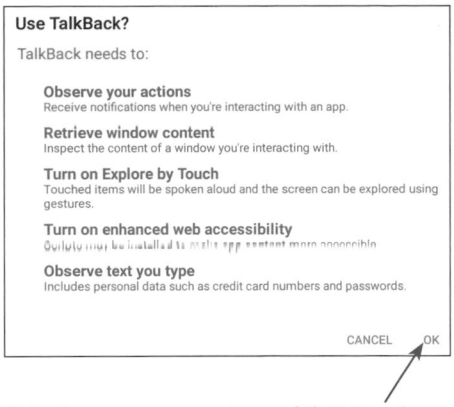

6 The active items are highlighted by a green, dotted box. Tap on an item to hear an audio description. Double-tap to activate a feature by touch

7 Tap on the **Magnification gestures** in Step 3 to access the setting for zooming on the screen by triple-tapping on it

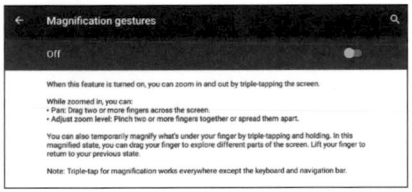

8 Drag this button On and triple tap on the screen to zoom in on what is being viewed

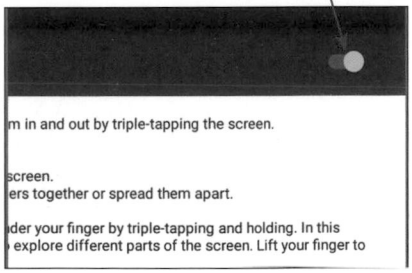

Tap on the **Touch & hold delay** button in Step 3 to select the time delay for an action to take effect when you press and hold on the screen or an icon.

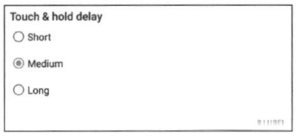

Security Issues

Security is a significant issue for all forms of computing and this is no different for Android tablet users. Three of the main areas of concern are:

- **Getting viruses from apps**. Android apps can contain viruses like any other computer programs but there are antivirus apps that can be used to try to detect viruses. Unlike programs on computers or laptops with file management systems, apps on a tablet tend to be more self-contained and do not interact with the rest of the system. This means that if they do contain viruses it is less likely that they will infect the whole tablet.

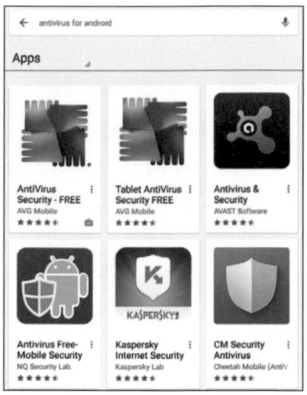

- **Losing your tablet or having it stolen**. If your tablet is lost or stolen you will want to try to get it back and also lock it remotely so that no-one else can gain access to your data and content. A lot of antivirus apps also contain a security function for lost or stolen devices.

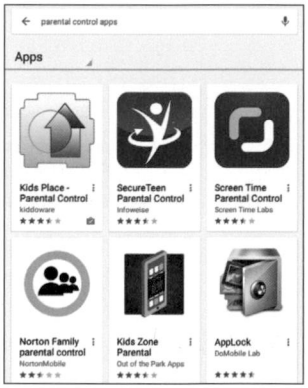

- **Restricting access for children**. If you have young children or grandchildren who are using your tablet you will want to know what they are using it for. This is particularly important for the Web, social media sites, video sharing sites and messaging sites where there is the potential to interact with other people. Restricted profiles can be used for children using your tablet (see page 176) and there is also a range of parental control apps that can be downloaded from the Play Store.

About Antivirus Apps

Android tablets are certainly not immune from viruses and malware and the FBI's Internet Crime Complaint Center (IC3) has even published advice and information about malicious software aimed at Android users. Some general precautions that can be taken to protect your tablet are:

- Use an antivirus app on your tablet. There are several of these and they can scan your tablet for any existing viruses and also check new apps and email attachments for potential problems.
- Apps that are provided in the Play Store are checked for viruses before they are published, but if you are in any doubt about an app, check it online before you download it. If you do an online search for the app, any issues related to it should be available.
- If you have a 3G or 4G connection, turn it off when you are not using it.
- Do not download any email attachments if you are not sure of their authenticity. If you do not know the person who has sent the email then delete it.

A lot of antivirus and security apps are free, but there is usually a Pro or Premium version that has to be paid for.

Functionality of antivirus apps

There are several antivirus apps available in the Play Store. Search for **android antivirus apps** (or similar) to view the apps. Most security apps have a similar range of features:

- **Scanning** for viruses and malicious software.
- **Online protection** against malicious software on websites.
- **Anti-theft protection.** This can be used to lock your tablet, locate it through location services, wipe its contents if they are particularly sensitive and instruct it to let out an alert sound.

For some of the functions of antivirus and security apps a sign-in is required, such as for the anti-theft options.

Some antivirus apps also have an option for backing up items, such as your contacts, which can then be restored to your tablet or another device if they are deleted or corrupted at all.

Using Antivirus Apps

Antivirus apps operate by scanning your tablet for malicious software. There are also usually options for displaying an activity log and additional tasks that are available.

It is worth downloading several of the free versions of antivirus apps, to see how you like them and to try the different functions that they have. You can use more than one antivirus app if you do not find all of the features you want in one app.

1. Open your antivirus app and tap on the **Protection** or **Scan** button

2. Details of the most recent scan are displayed. Tap on the **Scan** button to perform a new scan

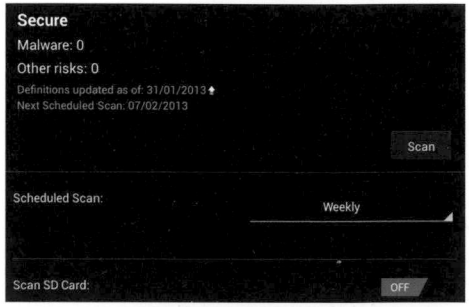

3. Tap in the **Scheduled Scan** box to specify a time period for when scans are performed automatically

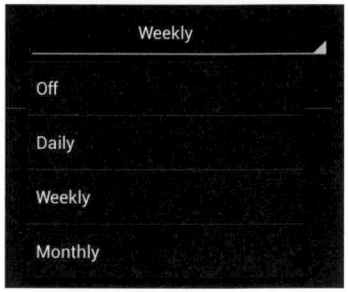

4. A countdown box shows the progress of the scan. This is where any results and actions are displayed

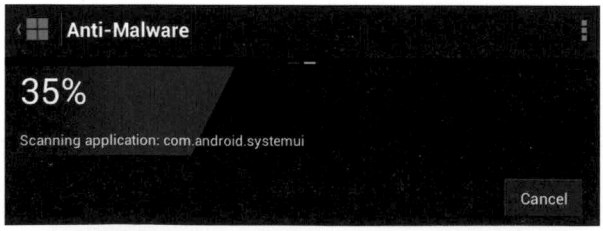

If any malicious software is found during a scan you will be given options for what you want to do with it, such as deleting it or quarantining it.

5 Tap on the app's menu (usually in the top right-hand corner) and tap on the **Activity Log** button, if there is one, to view tasks the app has performed

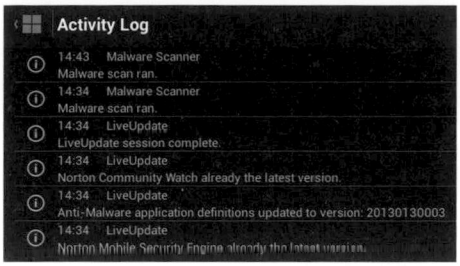

6 If there is a **Performance** option, tap on this to see the available items, including a **Task Killer**, that can be used to close down any unresponsive apps that are running

7 If there is a **Protection** option, tap on this to view additional scan options such as a **Deep File Scan** and **Safe Web Surfing**

If you have a free version of an antivirus app you will not have the full range of functionality, such as web protection and backup. However, the free versions should all perform a basic scan of your tablet.

The **Protection** and **Performance** options on this page are available in the **AVG AntiVirus** app; the **Activity Log** is from the **Norton Mobile Security** app.

Locating Your Tablet

The anti-theft function of antivirus and security apps can be used to locate your tablet if it is lost or stolen. This requires three elements to be in place:

- Location-based services has to be turned on, so that the anti-theft function can use this to locate it.
- You have to sign in to the app for the anti-theft functionality. This requires a username (usually your Google Account email address) and a password. These details are used to log in to the associated website (see next page).
- You need to have access to the website associated with the app. This is where you will locate your tablet and perform any other tasks as required.

To use the anti-theft function (this example is from the AVG AntiVirus app):

Some anti-theft apps have a test function whereby you can hear the sound alert that will be sent to it if it is lost.

1. Open your antivirus app and tap on the **Anti-Theft** button

2. You will have to register with your Google Account details. Enter these and tap on the **OK** button

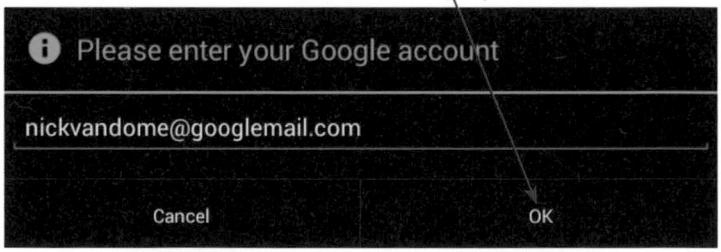

3 You will be sent an email with instructions on using the website for finding the location of your registered tablet. Click on the link in the email to go to the website, or

AVG | Anti-Theft

AVG Anti-Theft Instructions
Save this email in case your phone is ever lost

Hello,
Thank you for activating AVG Anti-Theft! If your phone or tablet is ever lost or stolen, please follow these instructions to remotely lock, wipe, or find it.

Your Android™ device: htc Nexus 9
Your SIM's serial number:
Your mobile operator:

Lost your phone or tablet?
Remotely lock, wipe, or find it in one of two ways

Note: For Anti-Theft to work, you'll need to first go to **Settings > Location services** on your device and make sure all services are on.

1 Via the Web
I. Click here to visit our Anti-Theft webpage.
II. Log in with your Google account: **nickvandome@googlemail.com**
III. Click your desired action

4 Click on the website link in the app

5 Log in to the website with your Google Account details

Most anti-theft apps have an option for wiping the data from a lost or stolen device. Only do this if you are worried about someone getting access to the content on your tablet and if you know it has been hacked up

...cont'd

6 Click on the **Locate** button. The website displays a map with your tablet's location. Click on the **Lock** button to remotely lock your tablet

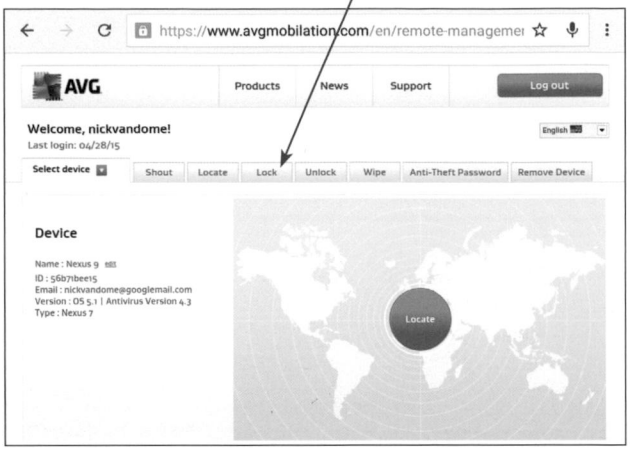

Click on the **Wipe** button in Step 6 to remotely delete the content on your tablet, if you are worried about it falling into the wrong hands.

7 Enter a **Lock Device** password. This will be used to unlock your tablet when you get it back. Tap on the **Next** button to complete the process

Symbols

3G/4G
  Connectivity 10, 20

A

AAC files 103
Accented letters.
  See Keyboard: Accented letters
Accessibility 178-179
  Explore by Touch 179
  Magnification gestures 179
Accessories 30
Address book 69
  See also Contacts app
All Apps button 32
Android 9
  Apps
    Interaction 19
  Overview 12
  Updating 13
  Version names 13
Anti-theft apps 181
Antivirus apps 181
  Using 182-183
Apple 9
Apps 9
  About 68
  Adding to the home screen 34
  Built-in 69-71
  Clear cache 80
  Clear data 80
  Deleting 78
  Disabling 78
  Downloading 76
  Finding 74-75
  Force stopping 80
  Information 80
  In the Play Store 72-73
  Moving 35
  New 72
  Searching for 75
  Updating 79
  Using 18-19, 68
Asus 21
Auto-correction 64
AVG AntiVirus 183

B

Back button 33
Background
  Changing 38
Battery 27
  Charging pack 30
  Consumption
    Saving 27
Bluetooth
  Sharing photos 132
Books
  Obtaining 114-115
Buttons
  Navigation 33

C

Calendar 144-145
Camera 26, 122
  For video calls 122
Caps lock 58
Chrome browser 149
Cleaning cloths 30
Cloud
  Saving items in 82
Connecting to the Internet
  With Wi-Fi 28, 44

Connectivity 10
Contacts app 22
  Adding contacts 143
  As an address book 142-143
Cookies 156
Cover 30

D

Dashboard.
  See Google Account: Dashboard
Dictionaries
  Adding to the keyboard 60
  Creating 66
Digital Rights Management. *See* DRM
Docking station 30
DRM 103

E

Ebooks
  Adding notes 118-119
  Around 116-117
  Bookmarks 120
  Definitions 121
  Deleting 116
  Reading controls 116
  Selecting text 118
  Table of contents 116
  Translations 121
Email 134.
  See also Gmail
Adding accounts 135-136
  Attachment security 181
  Manual setup 135
  Notifications 139
  Sending 138
  Settings 139
  Signature 139
  Using 137
  Viewing 137
Email app
  Superseded by Gmail 134
Events in a calendar 145

F

Facebook 140
Favorites 36
Favorites Tray 32, 36
FBI Internet Crime Complaint Center 181
File manager 84
Finding items 48-49
Folders
  Adding to the Favorites Tray 40
  Creating 40
Funamo 176

G

Getting around 33
Gift cards
  Redeeming 73
Gmail 134
  Adding accounts 135-136
  For numerous accounts 135
Going back 33
Google 13, 22, 48
Google+ 140
Google Account
  About 22
  Creating 24
  Dashboard 146
  Payment 22
  Using 146
Google Maps 70
Google Nexus 13, 20
Google Now
  About 52
  Cards 52
    Photo spot nearby 159
    Places 159

Public transport 159
Travel 159
Customizing 55
Gmail cards 53
When traveling 159
Google Play
Using 98
Google Search box 32, 48
Guest users 175

H

HDMI cable
For connecting to a TV 26, 113
Headphone jack 26
Headphones 105
Home button 33
Home screen 32
Moving between 33
Viewing 32
HTC 20
Hybrids 11

I

IC3. *See* FBI Internet Crime Complaint Center
Instagram 141
iOS 9
iPad 9
iTunes 103

J

Jelly Bean 13
JPEG file format
For photos 125

K

Keyboard
About 58-59
Accented letters 63
Add-on dictionaries 60
Advanced settings 61
Around 58-59
Auto-correction 61
Downloading additional 58
Dual functions 62
Hiding 59
Next word suggestions 61
Settings 60-61
Shortcuts 62-63
Show correction suggestions 61
Spacebar shortcut 63
Spell checker 60
Viewing 58
Kids Place 176
KitKat 13

L

Landscape mode 41
Levovo 21
Linux 12
Locating your tablet 184-186
Location-based services
For locating your tablet 184-186
Locking
Password 47
Pattern 47
PIN 47
Swipe 46
Your tablet 46-47
Lollipop 13
Losing your tablet 180

M

Malware 181
Managing
  Apps 19
Memory management 19
Microsoft 9
Micro USB port 26
Mobile data networks
  Using 3G and 4G 20
Mobile Wi-Fi unit 30
Movies 110-113
Movies and TV shows
  Renting 112
Multiple users
  Customization 171
  Overview 170-171
Music
  Artwork 101
  Clear queue 107
  Downloading
    From Play Store 100-101
  Managing 107
  On Android 99
  Pinning 108-109
  Playing 104-107
    Controls 106
  Sample content 100
  Transferring 102-104
    To Google Play 102-103
Music Manager 102
My Music
  On Google Play 103

N

Navigation 33
Navigation buttons 32
Near Field Communication. *See* NFC
Net Nanny 176
Nexus. *See* Google Nexus
NFC 44
Norton Family 176
Norton Mobile Security 183
Notifications 39
  Clearing 39
  Settings 39
  Viewing full details 39
Notifications area 39
Notifications bar 32, 39

O

Ok Google
  For voice search 51
Online protection 181
On/Off button 26
  For sleeping a tablet 26
Organizing apps 40

P

Parental control apps 176
Payment
  Through a Google Account 22
Photos
  Adding 124-126
  Cropping 131
  Editing 130-131
  From email 126
  Obtaining 124
  Sharing 132
  Transferring 125
  Viewing 127-129
Photos app 122-124
  For editing photos 130-131
  For viewing photos 127
Pinterest 141
Play Books 22, 114
Play Movies & TV 22, 110-113
Play Newsstand 22
Play Store 18, 22, 34
Portrait mode 41

Printer drivers 85
Printing 85

Q

Quick Settings 37, 47
QWERTY keyboard 59
  Adding numbers from 63

R

Recent apps button 33
Restricted profiles 176
Restricting access
  For children 176, 180
Rotating the screen 41
Routers
  For Wi-Fi access 28

S

Samsung Note 21
Samsung Tab 21
Scanning
  For malicious software 182-183
Screen lock 46-47
Screen protector 30
Screen rotation 41
  Locking 41
Searching 48-50
  Voice search 49-50
Security issues 180
Settings 43-45
  Accessing 43
  Accounts 45
  Device 44
  Personal 45
  System 45
  Wireless & Network 44
Setting up 28-29
  Apps & data 29
  Google Account 28
  Google Now 29
  Google services 29
  Language 28
  Wi-Fi 28
SIM card 26
Skype 164-165
Sleep mode 26
Smartphones 12
Snapchat 141
Social networking 140-141
Sony Experia 21
Spell checker 60, 64
Streaming 104
Stylus pen 30
Surface tablet 9
Swipe
  To unlock 46
Swiping
  On a web page 149

T

Tablets
  About 8-9
  Android operating system 9
  Models 20-21
Tablet terms
  Apps 15
  Camera 15
  Central Processing Unit (CPU) 14
  Connectivity 15
  Graphics card 15
  Memory 14
  Operating System 15
  Ports 15
  Processor 14
  Random-access memory (RAM) 14
  Sensors 15
  Storage 14

Touchscreen 15
Wireless 15
TalkBack 178-179
Task killer 183
Text
Adding 64
Copy and paste 65
Selecting 65
Text size 178
Touchscreen 10
Using 16-17
Traveling
Hotels 162
TripAdvisor 162
Tumblr 141
Turning on 26, 28
TV shows 110-113
Twitter 140-141

U

UNESCO 168
USB adapter 30
USB cable 27
USB port 26
Users
Switching between 174

V

Videos
Personal
Adding 124
Virtual Private Network. *See* VPN
Viruses 180
Volume button 26
VPN 44

W

Wake up
From sleep 26
Wallpaper 38
Wallpaper apps
Downloading 38
Web browsers
Android 148
Web pages
Navigating around 149
Websites
Bookmarking pages 150-151
Browser settings 155-156
Images 152
Incognito browsing 154
Links 152
Mobile versions 148
Opening pages 149
Private browsing 154
Tabs 153
Welcome screen 173
Widgets
Adding 37
Windows 10 9
Wiping data 185
World Heritage sites 168

Y

YouTube 112, 141

Z

Zooming in and out
On web pages 149